Accounting for Corporations: Volume Two

by Therese Trainor

DARNLEY
PUBLISHING
GROUP

ISBN 978-2-923623-69-6

Printed in Canada

Catalog No. TAAC6

Senior Reviewer: Stanley Mroz
Editor-in-chief: Ernest Smith, Ph.D.
Senior Editor: Joanne Labre
Design and Cover: Saskia Nieuwendijk

IV

Accounting for Corporations

Table of Contents

Chapter One - Carrying Current Assets

The Reason for This Chapter

Accounting does not limit the number of accounts used by any business. Thankfully, the same types of accounts tend to exist for all businesses. For reporting purposes, these similarities allow us to classify accounts in an organized manner.

At the end of each accounting cycle we close out the temporary account balances. The permanent balances continue to exist. But for how long? Some accounts continue living for a longer period than others.

Do account values remain stable over time? Not all. Some account values change periodically. The users of financial statements appreciate knowing the carrying of up-to-date values of these accounts. Therefore, understanding the nature of accounts is paramount in any attempt to classify them.

This chapter deals with assets expected to have a short life. First, we define which assets fall into this category. Next, we examine one such asset in greater detail - temporary investments.

What Do You Already Know?

In this section of the chapter we ask you to complete a pre-test. It will get you thinking about what you already know about accounting. It will also ensure you have the required knowledge to understand the contents of this chapter. After completing the pre-test, check your answers against the ones provided.

Pre-Test

Question One

Describe the process used to determine the dollar value reported on the balance sheet for the cash account.

Question Two

Describe the process used to determine the dollar value reported on the balance sheet for the accounts receivable account.

Answers to Pre-Test

Answer to Question One

The dollar value of the cash account reported on the balance sheet must match its ledger balance for the same day. For example, if on December 31, 2014, the cash ledger balance shows $2,340.00 then this must be the amount shown on the December 31, 2014 balance sheet. Otherwise, the accounts do not balance.

The amount of cash reported, in this example $2,340.00, reflects the sum of all cash available. That is, money in the bank accounts, petty cash, IOU's from employees etc. are added together to determine the cash amount. Periodically, the company's cash ledger is reconciled to the bank statement. Usually this takes place once a month, when the bank statement is received. The reconciliation process may require journal entries and posting to the cash ledger in order to bring the cash account up to date.

Because cash transactions are often quite numerous, most companies will keep special journals and subsidiary ledgers to help control the cash account. A complete review of these topics can be found in Volume Three of this series. Chapters One and Two cover special journals and ledgers while Chapter Four examines the reconciliation process.

Answer to Question Two

The dollar value of the accounts receivable account reported on the balance sheet must match its ledger balance for the same day. For example, if on December 31, 2014, the accounts receivable account ledger balance shows $15,980.00, then this must be the amount shown on the December 31, 2014, balance sheet. Otherwise, the accounts do not balance and the error must be found.

The amount of receivables reported, in this example $15,980.00 on December 31, 2014, reflects the total amount of what is owed and likely to be repaid by customers and other debtors. The reported amount may equal the outstanding credit sales. More likely, the accountant adjusts the credit sales figure by an amount estimated to be uncollectible. Recall, the Accounts Receivable amount on the balance sheet is reduced by the contra account Allowance for Doubtful Accounts to reflect the amount of receivables expected to be collected. We refer to the resulting net amount as the Carrying Value. Details of this topic can be found in Volume Two, Chapter Five of this series.

Because such transactions are often quite numerous, most companies will keep special journals and subsidiary ledgers to help control the accounts receivable account. A complete review of this topic can be found in Volume Three of this series. Chapters One and Two cover special journals and ledgers.

How This Chapter Relates to Other Chapters in This Book

This book provides instruction on how to classify and value the permanent or balance sheet accounts commonly reported by corporations. This process requires that we group accounts according to how long we expect them to last. The first two chapters examine short-lived assets that will probably experience changing values. The third provides a review. Chapter Four looks at assets that are expected to exist for a longer period. Chapter Five inspects and divides liabilities into two groups: short-term and long-term. It also introduces a new equity classification: preferred shares. We conclude this book with a review; Chapter Six.

What Are the Topics in This Chapter?

What are current assets? At what value do we carry them on the balance sheet? This chapter begins by defining current assets. It lists the common current assets along with instructions on reporting their carrying values. However, we devote the bulk of the chapter to exploring a new current asset account, Temporary Investments.

Topics Covered in Chapter One	*Level of Importance*
What Are Current Assets?	
Definition	***
The Operating Cycle	***
What Is Liquidity?	***
The Carrying Value	***
Ordering Current Assets by Liquidity	***
Temporary Investments	
The Need for Temporary Investments	**
The Nature of Temporary Investments	***
Temporary Investments Defined	***
Measuring Temporary Investments	
The Cost Principle, Again	**
An Exception to the Cost Principle	***
Basic Accounting for Temporary Investments	
The Basic Transaction	***
Receiving Income	***
Realizing a Gain	***
Realizing a Loss	***

Topics Covered in Chapter One	*Level of Importance*
Understanding Lower of Cost and Market (LCM)	
Unrealized Holding Gain	***
Unrealized Holding Loss	***
Using Lower of Cost and Market (LCM)	
For One Security	**
For Many Securities	**

Legend

*	indicates a low level of importance
**	indicates a medium level of importance
***	indicates a high level of importance

What Are Current Assets?

Definition

Current assets are those assets we expect to convert into cash or use up within one year from the balance sheet date or during the operating cycle of the business, whichever is longer. Therefore cash is a current asset. In order to classify other assets as current, you must understand the nature of both the operating cycle and liquidity. We will examine each in turn.

The Operating Cycle

Typically, the nature of a business repeats itself. The same process is followed over and over within some time period. For example, a merchandise company uses cash to purchase goods that are held in inventory until sold on credit. The credit sales are collected replenishing the cash account. The operating cycle reflects the circular motion of typical transactions in operating the business, starting with cash and ending with cash. We depict it in the following diagram:

<u>Typical Operating Cycle</u>

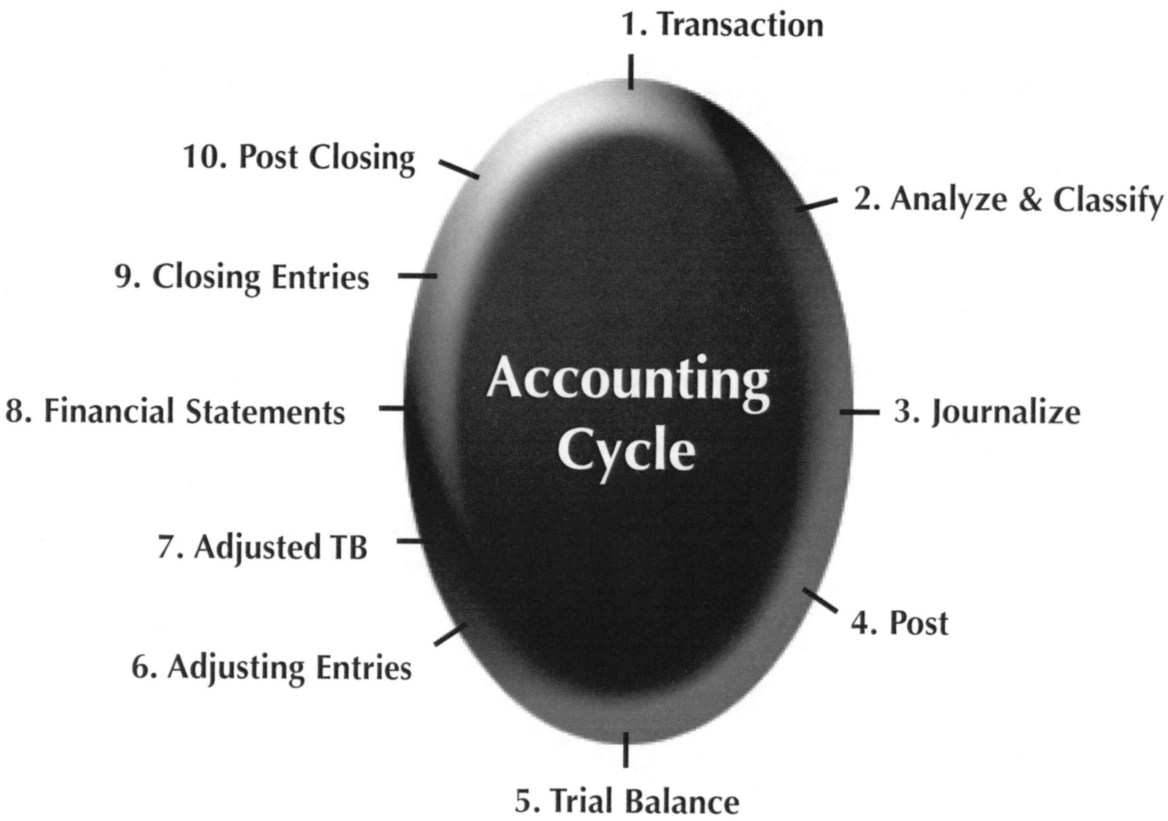

For most companies the operating cycle is less than one year. Current assets are those expected to be in existence for one year or the operating cycle, whichever is greater. An attractive feature of current assets is their liquidity.

What Is Liquidity?

Liquidity refers to the ease with which assets can be converted into cash. We deem assets to be liquid if we can sell them quickly without suffering a loss in value. For example, do you think your car is liquid? Probably not. You could sell it quickly, but at what price?

Current assets are liquid. This means we expect they will be converted into cash or used up within the operating cycle **and** that they should maintain their value reasonably well. That is, no huge losses or gains should be anticipated on the disposal of current assets. Liquidity requires both the speed and value elements.

Some current assets keep their value better than others. We carry the current assets on the balance sheet in their order of liquidity.

The Carrying Value

We report the value of all assets on the balance sheet at an amount that best reflects their cash-equivalent value. Determining this carrying value becomes increasingly important, and complicated, the less liquid an asset is. This book is a study of how to carry assets. This chapter discusses carrying current assets except for inventory, which is the topic of the next chapter.

Ordering Current Assets by Liquidity

Accountants make an earnest effort to list each business' current assets in order of their liquidity. While the ordered list may differ between any two companies, in general it looks like this:

Cash. The most liquid of all assets because no conversion to cash is needed. It already is. We carry cash at its face value on the balance sheet. A review is provided in the Self-Test, Question One.

Temporary Investments. An account used to invest idle cash for a short period of time.

Accounts Receivable. The credit sale has been made, we now await the cash. While many different terms of sale exist, businesses usually expect their customers to pay accounts within thirty days. Thus, receivables should be converted into cash within this time. However, not all credit sales will be repaid. Generally, the carrying value of receivables includes an allowance for doubtful accounts. A review is provided in the Self-Test, Question Two.

Inventory. The goods have been purchased, but not yet sold. The liquidity of inventory may be very different from business to business. However, the majority of companies take longer than 30 days to sell their goods, so we list inventory after receivables. As the carrying value of inventory is quite a complex topic, we devote Chapter Two to it.

Prepaid Operating Costs and Other Receivables. Prepaids include items such as prepaid insurance, rent, etc. Other Receivables are usually tied to investment revenue such as Dividend or Interest Revenue Receivable. The listing of these accounts depends on how long they are expected to remain open. We use adjusting entries to account for these accruals and deferrals. Volume Two, Chapter One of this series is a study of adjusting entries.

Students should note this list is not exhaustive. We have provided the most common current asset accounts, only.

Now You Try It

Learning Exercise One

The bookkeeper for Jumble Incorporated doesn't know how to list the accounts on the balance sheet. On December 31, 2014 he provided you with a jumbled record of selected ledger accounts and their amounts, as follows:

Account Name	Amount ($)
Land	25,000
Retained Earnings	198,250
Allowance for Doubtful Accounts	5,420
Temporary Investments	12,845
Building	78,000
Inventory	45,488
Cash	3,330
Notes Payable	12,000
Accounts Receivable	22,450
Common Shares	230,000
Prepaid Insurance	4,500

Use the space provided below to prepare the current asset section, in good form, of the December 31, 2014 balance sheet for Jumble Incorporated.

____

____

____

TOTAL CURRENT ASSETS	

Answers

Answer to Learning Exercise One

Jumble Incorporated
Balance Sheet (current asset portion)
As at December 31, 2014

Cash		$ 3,330
Accounts Receivable	$22,450	
Less: Allowance for Doubtful Accounts	(5,420)	
Carrying value of Receivables		17,030
Inventory		45,488
Temporary Investments		12,845
Prepaid Insurance		4,500
TOTAL CURRENT ASSETS		$83,193

Temporary Investments

We have defined Temporary Investments (also known as Short-term Investments) as an account used to invest idle cash. We devote the remainder of this chapter to its study. We begin the discussion by considering the need and nature of these investments, followed by a suitable definition.

The Need for Temporary Investments

Money placed at the bank in a corporate checking account tends to earn little or no interest. This lost opportunity can prove quite costly. When a business produces cash that temporarily has no productive use, it should invest that cash in a temporary investment. Money invested in a short-term security may provide a return, yet remain liquid.

The Nature of Temporary Investments

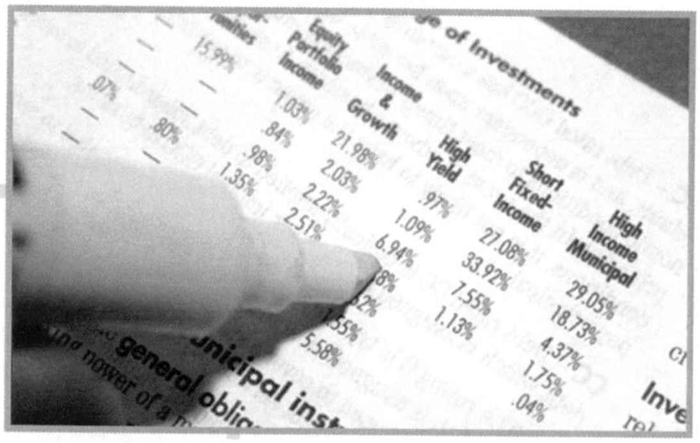

Many different types of securities exist. Some offer interest, such as government and corporate bonds. Others, such as stocks, offer dividends. With such a wide variety of investment products, many different maturity dates and holding periods are available. Management should select securities that are most suitable for their temporary investment needs. This requires special expertise and is considered too advanced for our discussion. However, we must realize it is better to generate interest or dividends than allow cash to remain idle.

Short-term or temporary investments are not defined by the particular investment securities chosen. Rather, the length of time the investment will be held determines whether it should be classified as a short-term investment. The nature of these investments dictates that cash is idle only temporarily and will be needed in the not too distant future. Thus, when idle cash will be invested for a long period of time it should not be classified as a short-term investment. In order to fit within the definition of a current asset, the holding period of a temporary investment cannot be longer than the greater of the operating cycle or one year.

When management's intent is to invest non-productive cash for periods longer than the current asset classification permits, the investment should not be recognized as a temporary investment in the current asset section of the balance sheet. In such a case long-term investments should be classified as such and reported in their own balance sheet section.

Temporary Investments Defined

To classify an investment as temporary, two principles should be satisfied. Firstly, the intended holding period cannot exceed the greater of the operating cycle or one year. Satisfying this requirement allows us to classify the account as a current asset. Secondly, the investment should be marketable. This means it can be sold with ease reasonably quick. Securities traded on organized exchanges, such as a stock exchange have marketability. This also satisfies the requirement that current assets should be liquid. Because temporary or short-term investments should be marketable the account is sometimes named marketable securities. All three terms refer to the same type of account.

Measuring Temporary Investments

The Cost Principle, Again

Initially, we record the purchase of short-term investments at their acquisition cost. This is in conformance with the cost principle. The acquisition cost includes any fees, commissions or taxes associated with the transaction. When the investment earns interest or declares a dividend, we report the revenue as such.

Now You Try It

Learning Exercise Two

On November 5, 2014, NoNeed Limited invested $5,000 of idle cash in a security. The brokerage fee for the transaction was $50. Management intends to sell the security within the next three months. On November 30, 2014 the security earned $45 worth of interest and the cash was received. Show the journal entries needed to record these transactions. Use the space provided below:

NoNeed Limited - General Journal

Date	Debit $	Credit $

Date	Debit $	Credit $

Answers

Answer to Learning Exercise Two

NoNeed Limited - General Journal

Date *November 5, 2014*	*Debit $*	*Credit $*
Temporary Investment	*5,050*	
Cash		*5,050*
To record the purchase of a temporary investment for $5,000 plus fee of $50.		

Date *November 30, 2014*	*Debit $*	*Credit $*
Cash	*45*	
Interest Revenue		*45*
To record interest earned on a temporary investment.		

An Exception to the Cost Principle

When the value of a security declines below its acquisition cost, the balance sheet no longer reflects the value of the temporary investment. An adjustment should be made to reflect the change in value. The temporary investment is carried at its market value, not its acquisition cost. This rule is known as Lower of Cost and Market (LCM). We use it to report the carrying value of temporary investments.

Using LCM agrees with the notion it is better to err on the side of conservatism. That is, it is better to provide for all losses but anticipate no profits. When the value of securities has dropped we report the lower amount. If they rise in value, we do not report the profit until it is secure. The next two sections cover these ideas in greater detail

Basic Accounting for Temporary Investments

The Basic Transaction

If the value of the underlying security does not change, accounting for Temporary Investments is relatively straightforward. The company simply debits the Temporary Investments account when securities are purchased and credits it when they are sold. We offset the transactions using the cash account. As demonstrated in Learning Exercise Two, the cost of the purchase should include any fees or broker's commissions incurred.

Receiving Income

When the short-term investment earns income, we report it on the income statement. As always, we use the accrual system of accounting. That is, we report revenues when earned and expenses when incurred. Therefore, the company reports any interest revenue on investments when it is earned, and dividend revenue when the associated dividend is declared.

Recall that under a cash-based accounting system, we would report transactions only when the actual cash is exchanged. Worldwide, the exclusive use of cash-based systems is rare.

Realizing a Gain

If a short-term investment is sold to yield a profit, we report the gain on the income statement at the time it is realized. In fact, gains are only reported once the securities are sold or "realized". Therefore, both the income and gains resulting from a temporary investment are shown on the income statement, but separately.

When the securities are sold, a credit is made to reduce the temporary investments account. The credit amount depends on the carrying value of the temporary securities. We cover this process in the "Understanding Lower of Cost and Market" section, later on. For now, we simply use the acquisition value and report a gain if the cash received from the sale exceeds the acquisition value.

Now You Try It

Learning Exercise Three

On August 3, 2014, Berger Corporation invested $9,600 of idle cash by purchasing 200 shares of Atalis Corporation. This amount includes the brokerage commission. Management estimated they would need the cash from this investment by the end of December.

On both September 5 and December 5, Atalis Corporation declared a dividend of $0.48 per share. A $96 check was received by Berger Corporation on October 3 for the dividend declared on September 5. The check for the dividend declared on December 5 has not yet been received. On December 23, 2014, Berger sold all 200 shares of its investment in Atalis at a price of $53 each. Assume that Berger Corporation was entitled to keep the full dividend payment received in October.

Show the journal entries Berger Corporation would make to record these transactions. Use the space provided below:

Berger Corporation - General Journal

Date	Debit $	Credit $

Computations:

Date	Debit $	Credit $

Date	Debit $	Credit $

Date	Debit $	Credit $

Date	Debit $	Credit $

Computations:

Answers

Answer to Learning Exercise Three

Berger Corporation - General Journal

Date *August 3, 2014*	***Debit $***	***Credit $***
Temporary Investment	*9,600*	
Cash		*9,600*
To record the purchase of 200 shares of Atalis Corporation for $48 each, to be held temporarily.*		

Computations:

**$9,600 ÷ 200 = $48*

Date *September 5, 2014*	***Debit $***	***Credit $***
Dividend Revenue Receivable	*96*	
Dividend Revenue		*96*
To record a $0.48 per share dividend declared on 200 shares of Atalis Corporation.		

Date *October 3, 2014*	***Debit $***	***Credit $***
Cash	*96*	
Dividend Revenue Receivable		*96*
To record payment of the $0.48 per share dividend declared on 200 shares of Atalis Corporation.		

Date December 5, 2014	**Debit $**	**Credit $**
Dividend Revenue Receivable	96	
Dividend Revenue		96
To record a $0.48 per share dividend declared on 200 shares of Atalis Corporation.		

Date December 23, 2014	**Debit $**	**Credit $**
Cash	10,600*	
Temporary Investment		9,600
Gain on Sale of Temporary Investment		1,000**
To record a $1,000 gain on disposal of 200 shares of Atalis Corporation, at $53 each.		

Computations:

*200 x $53 = $10,600

**$53 - $48 = $5 gain per share. $5 x 200 = $1,000

Realizing a Loss

If a loss is incurred on the disposal of temporary investments, it will be recognized on the income statement as such. We follow the same process as with making a gain. However, where a gain results in a credit, or addition to income on the income statement, the loss will result in a debit, or reduction to income. We should also note that gains and losses resulting from the disposal of securities have income tax implications, none of which will be explored here.

Now You Try It

Learning Exercise Four

The following prices were available for Corporal Corporation's shares:

Date	Price per Share
March 2, 2014	$25
April 1, 2014	$27
May 3, 2014	$20

The management of My Company purchased 300 shares of Corporal Corporation on March 2, 2014 and sold them on May 3, 2014. No dividends were declared in the interim. Prepare the necessary journal entries for My Company to record these transactions, using the space provided below:

My Company - General Journal

Date	Debit $	Credit $

Computations:

Date	Debit $	Credit $

Computations:

Answers

Answer to Learning Exercise Four

My Company - General Journal

Date March 2, 2014	**Debit $**	**Credit $**
Temporary Investment	7,500*	
Cash		7,500
To record the purchase of 300 shares of Corporal Corporation at $25 each.		

Computations:

*300 x $25 = $7,500

Date May 3, 2014	**Debit $**	**Credit $**
Cash	6,000*	
Temporary Investment		7,500
Loss on Sale of Temporary Investment	1,500**	
To record a $1,500 loss on disposal of 300 shares of Corporal Corporation, at $20 each.		

Computations:

*300 x $20 = $6,000

**$25 - $20 = $5 loss per share, 300 x $5 = $1,500 loss.

Notice in the preceding examples, all the securities were sold when realizing a loss or gain. This need not be so. Management may decide to sell all or any portion of the securities. We must account for the actual transaction, as in Learning Exercise Five.

Now You Try It

Learning Exercise Five

The following prices were available for the shares of Fennel Kennels Inc.:

Date	Price per Share
June 1, 2014	$15
July 31, 2014	$10

The management of Your Company purchased 400 shares on June 1, 2014 and sold 200 of them on July 31, 2014. No dividends were declared during the interim period. Prepare the necessary journal entries for Your Company to record these transactions, using the space provided below:

Your Company - General Journal

Date	Debit $	Credit $

Computations:

Date	Debit $	Credit $

Computations:

Answers

Answer to Learning Exercise Five

Your Company - General Journal

Date *June 1, 2014*	**Debit $**	**Credit $**
Temporary Investment	*6,000**	
Cash		*6,000*
To record the purchase of 400 shares of Fennel Kennels Inc. at $15 each.		

Computations:

**400 x $15 = $6,000*

Date *July 31, 2014*	**Debit $**	**Credit $**
Cash	*2,000**	
Temporary Investment		*3,000***
Realized Loss on Sale of Temporary Investment	*1,000****	
To record a $1,000 loss on disposal of 200 shares of Fennel Kennels Inc., at $10 each.		

Computations:

*200 x $10 = $2,000

** 200 x $15 = $3,000

***$15 - $10 = $5 loss per share, 200 x $5 = $1,000 loss.

We reduced the temporary investments by the acquisition cost ($15) of the 200 shares sold. However, the temporary investments account is not closed. The company still has 200 shares of Fennel Kennels. We must carry these remaining shares at the lower of cost and market. We demonstrate this, next.

Understanding Lower of Cost and Market (LCM)

Unrealized Holding Gain

Security prices change often. They may increase or decrease by any amount. Thus, the value of temporary investments will probably fluctuate over time. When the security's price rises, yet it is not sold, we have made a gain from holding it. However, this gain can not be "realized" or locked in until the sale takes place. At any time before the sale, the gain could be diminished or even turned into a loss. Because this unrealized gain is not secure, we do not report it. To do so would be optimistic and not qualify as "good" accounting. It would not be conservative.

Unrealized Holding Loss

Conservative accounting practice dictates the use of LCM. It is the essence of "good" accounting. When a security's value has diminished, yet we continue to hold it, the acquisition value no longer represents its worth. There has been a loss. Although it has not been "realized" or locked in, the carrying value of temporary investments is overstated. To inform financial statement readers of the decline in value, we record unrealized holding losses. Doing so reduces the carrying value of temporary investments to a more realistic amount.

To recap, the central idea is to provide for all losses but anticipate no profits. When the value of securities drops, we report the loss in value. If the securities rise in value, we do not report the profit until the securities have been sold and the gain is secure. Therefore we report **all realized** gains and losses, but only **unrealized holding losses**. It may be noted that in practice, many companies will recognize an unrealized holding gain, up to the original cost of the securities, if the market value of securities previously written down to LCM has recovered. Discussion of this somewhat complex accounting procedure is beyond the scope of this course.

Using Lower of Cost and Market (LCM)

For One Security

We carry the temporary investment at the lower of cost and market. As previously discussed, when an unrealized holding gain occurs, we ignore it. When an unrealized holding loss occurs, we prepare the following journal entry:

Debit	*Unrealized Holding Loss on Temporary Investment*
Credit	*Temporary Investment*

For the amount of the unrealized holding loss. This entry writes down the carrying value of the temporary investment on the balance sheet and shows an unrealized loss on the income statement.

Instead of writing down the temporary investment directly, an alternative approach may be used. The unrealized holding loss may be credited to a contra asset account "Allowance to Reduce Temporary Investments to Market". Sometimes similar account names are used instead. This allowance valuation process is identical to the Allowance for Doubtful accounts method used to reduce Accounts Receivable. The attractiveness of this valuation allowance technique comes from its preservation of the original account information for the temporary investment.

In the interests of simplicity, this book writes off unrealized holding losses against the temporary investments account, directly. However, the process of crediting the contra asset account, Allowance to Reduce Temporary Investments to Market, is more widely used in conjunction with the portfolio approach. We discuss this briefly at the end of the learning section.

Now You Try It

Learning Exercise Six

Let's conclude the necessary transactions for Your Company from Learning Exercise Five. For your convenience, we repeat the information, below:

The following prices were available for the shares of Fennel Kennels Inc.:

Date	Price per Share
June 1, 2014	$15
July 31, 2014	$10

The management of Your Company purchased 400 shares on June 1, 2014 and sold 200 of them on July 31, 2014. No dividends were declared in the interim. You have already prepared the journal entries. We repeat them below:

Your Company - General Journal

Date *June 1, 2014*	Debit $	Credit $
Temporary Investment	6,000*	
Cash		6,000
To record the purchase of 400 shares of Fennel Kennels Inc. at $15 each.		

Date *July 31, 2014*	Debit $	Credit $
Cash	2,000*	
Temporary Investment		3,000**
Realized Loss on Sale of Temporary Investment	1,000***	
To record a $1,000 loss on disposal of 200 shares of Fennel Kennels Inc., at $10 each.		

Now, prepare the journal entries needed to restate the carrying value of the Temporary Investment to lower of cost and market on July 31, 2014. Use the space provided below:

Your Company - General Journal

Date	Debit $	Credit $

Computations:

Next, post the journal entries of June 1 and July 31, 2014 to the ledger. We have provided space below.

Your Company - General Journal

Cash

Temporary Investment

Realized Loss on Sale of Temporary Investment

Unrealized Holding Loss on Temporary Investment

Lastly, what is the carrying value of the Temporary Investment on July 31, 2014? Why is it correct?

____

____

____

____

Answers

Answer to Learning Exercise Six

Your Company - General Journal

Date July 31, 2014	**Debit $**	**Credit $**
Unrealized Holding Loss on Temporary Investment	1,000	
Temporary Investment		1,000
To record the unrealized holding loss on 200 shares of Fennel Kennels Inc. now valued at $10 each.		

Computations:

*200 x ($15 - $10) = $1,000

Your Company - General Journal

Cash

Debit	Credit
	6,000
2,000	
	4,000

Temporary Investment

Debit	Credit
6,000	
	3,000
	1,000
2,000	

Realized Loss on Sale of Temporary Investment

Debit	Credit
1,000	

Unrealized Holding Loss on Temporary Investment

Debit	Credit
1,000	

The balance in the Cash account may appear strange (a credit), but remember we have only shown a few transactions in this exercise.

The carrying value of the Temporary Investment is now $2,000. This is correct because on July 31, 2014, Your Company has 200 shares of Fennel Kennels and each share is worth $10. Thus, 200 x $10 = $2,000, the value in the Temporary Investment account.

Your company purchased 400 shares at $15 each for a total of $6,000. The 400 shares dropped in value by $5 each for a total loss of $2,000 (400 x $5 = $2,000). Since 200 shares were actually sold for $10 each, half of the loss was realized ($1,000) while the other half remains unrealized.

For Many Securities

Thus far we have invested idle cash in one security, only. In reality a company may have investments in several different securities at any one time. Together, these securities form a portfolio. Regardless of the number of securities held, we carry temporary investments at the lower of cost and market.

Two approaches exist for carrying portfolio investments at the lower of cost and market. In the first instance, we account for unrealized holding losses on a security by security basis. This is the method we follow in this chapter. The second method uses an aggregate or portfolio approach. To satisfy LCM, it requires adjustment to the entire portfolio, using some contra asset account like "Allowance to Reduce Temporary Investments to Market", rather than security by security. While the approach may require less bookkeeping, it is conceptually more difficult to follow. We will not cover it here.

Now You Try it

Learning Exercise Seven

Wanton Limited invested their idle cash on April 1, 2014, for one year. On that date it purchased 100 shares in each of three companies (for a total of 300 shares). The activity of these stocks during 2014, is shown in the table below:

Share	Acquisition Cost ($)	Price on June 30, 2014	Price on Sept. 30, 2014	Price on Dec. 31, 2014
Alpha Inc.	5,000	49	52	50
Beta Inc.	3,000	32	29	30
Charlie Inc.	2,000	20	18	20
TOTAL	$10,000			

The company prepares its financial statements quarterly, with a December 31, 2014 year-end. Use the space provided below to record all the necessary journal entries for the year 2014. On December 31, 2014 what is the carrying value of the temporary investments of Wanton Limited?

Wanton - General Journal

Date	Debit	Credit

Computations:

Date	Debit	Credit

Computations:

Date	Debit	Credit

Computations:

Date	Debit	Credit

Computations:

Date	Debit	Credit

Computations:

Date	Debit	Credit

Computations:

Answers

Answer to Learning Exercise Seven

Wanton - General Journal

Date April 1, 2014	**Debit**	**Credit**
Temporary Investments	5,000	
Cash		5,000
To record the purchase of 100 Alpha Inc. shares at $50 each.		

Computations:

*$5,000 ÷100 = $50 per share

Date April 1, 2014	**Debit**	**Credit**
Temporary Investments	3,000	
Cash		3,000
To record the purchase of 100 Beta Inc. shares at $30 each.		

Computations:

*$3,000 ÷100 = $30 per share

Date April 1, 2014	**Debit**	**Credit**
Temporary Investments	2,000	
Cash		2,000
To record the purchase of 100 Charlie Inc. shares at $20 each.		

Computations:

*$2,000 ÷100 = $20 per share

Date June 30, 2014	**Debit**	**Credit**
Unrealized Holding Loss on Temporary Investment	100	
Temporary Investment		100
To record the unrealized holding loss on 100 shares of Alpha Inc. now valued at $49 each.		

Computations:

*100 x ($50 - $49) = $100

Date *September 30, 2014*	***Debit***	***Credit***
Unrealized Holding Loss on Temporary Investment	*100*	
Temporary Investment		*100*
To record the unrealized holding loss on 100 shares of Beta Inc. now valued at $29 each.		

Computations:

**100 x ($30 - $29) = $100*

Date *September 30, 2014*	***Debit***	***Credit***
Unrealized Holding Loss on Temporary Investment	*200*	
Temporary Investment		*200*
To record the unrealized holding loss on 100 shares of Charlie Inc. now valued at $18 each.		

Computations:

**100 x ($20 - $18) = $200*

As none of the shares have been sold, any change in value must be due to holding the securities. To satisfy LCM, the value of each security will be marked down at the end of the accounting period, if its market price has fallen. As no unrealized holding gains can be captured, the securities will be carried at its lowest price during the year. On December 31, 2014, the security prices have returned to their acquisition cost. However, these temporary securities will be carried at their lowest value, as follows:

Security	**Acquisition Cost ($)**	**Unrealized Holding Loss ($)**	**Carrying Value ($)**
Alpha Inc.	5,000	100	4,900
Beta Inc.	3,000	100	2,900
Charlie Inc.	2,000	200	1,800
TOTAL	10,000	400	9,600

Should any gains be realized, they will be reported at the time of sale.

What You Have Learned in This Chapter

This chapter classifies certain assets as current. The operating cycle helps us distinguish assets falling into this category. We list current assets in order of their liquidity. This requires an understanding of two elements: speed, or how quickly are the assets used or converted into cash and loss of value.

Chapter One explored the carrying values of current assets. It considered a new current asset, Temporary Investments. This investigation yielded a new concept; Lower of Cost and Market. It serves to remind us that good accounting practice falls on the side of conservatism. Thus, we report realized gains and losses and unrealized losses, but never unrealized gains.

Reviewing the section "Important Terms in this Chapter" provides a great summary. It serves to test your understanding. If you can define all these terms, you most likely have a good grasp of the topics covered. You will further test this knowledge by completing the Self-Test and Practice Problems. Good Luck.

Important Terms in This Chapter

Accrual System of Accounting: report revenues when earned and expenses when incurred, regardless of when cash is actually exchanged.

Allowance for Doubtful Accounts: a contra asset account used in conjunction with Bad Debt Expense to estimate the value of receivables that will not be collected. It reduces reported accounts receivable to its appropriate carrying value.

Carrying Value: the dollar value used to report an account on the balance sheet. The method selected should best reflect the asset's cash-equivalent value.

Current Assets: those assets we expect to convert into cash or use up within one year from the balance sheet date or during the operating cycle of the business, whichever is longer.

Liquidity: the ease with which assets can be converted into cash. We deem assets to be liquid if we can sell them quickly without suffering a loss in value. Current assets are listed in order of their liquidity.

Lower of Cost and Market (LCM): when the value of a security declines below its acquisition cost we adjust the balance sheet to carry the security at its market value.

Marketable Securities: an account used to invest idle cash for a short period of time.

Other Receivables: receivables other than Accounts Receivable. Typical examples include Interest or Dividend Revenue Receivable.

Operating Cycle: reflects the circular motion of typical transactions in operating the business, starting with cash and ending with cash.

Portfolio: an investment consisting of several different securities.

Prepaid Operating Costs: also known as the prepaids; such as prepaid insurance, rent, etc. At the end of each accounting period, we make adjusting entries to reduce these current asset accounts for the portion consumed (used up) during the period.

Realized Gain: the sale of a security at a price greater than the acquisition cost. The difference is the realized gain and is reported.

Realized Loss: the sale of a security at a price below the acquisition cost. The difference is the realized loss and is reported.

Short-term Investments: see marketable securities

Temporary Investments: see marketable securities

Unrealized Gain: the increase in value of a security above its acquisition cost. The difference is the unrealized gain and is not reported.

Unrealized Loss: the decrease in value of a security below its current carrying value (originally the acquisition cost). The decline is an unrealized loss and is reported.

Write down: to reduce.

Should You Move on to the Next Chapter?

It's time to see if you are comfortable with your new knowledge. Complete the Self-Test and Practice Problems to determine whether or not you are ready to move on to the next Chapter.

Self-Test for Chapter One

Question One

Create a list showing the correct order of current assets. Justify the ordering.

Question Two

You work in a bookstore that grants its customers 30 days to pay for sales on credit. If the operating cycle for the business is 120 days, what do the other 90 days represent?

Question Three

When a company invests in the shares of another company, the investment could last for many years. Under what circumstances should we consider this investment to be temporary?

Question Four

The following market prices were available for the shares of Mayhem Ltd.:

Date	Price per Share
October 18, 2014	$32
November 11, 2014	$30
December 29, 2014	$28
January 8, 2015	$25 (expected)

The management of Luso Company purchased 1,000 Mayhem shares on October 1, 2014 for $33 each. On November 11, 2014 the management of Luso Company sold 300 shares at the market price. On December 5, 2014, Mayhem Ltd. declared a $0.78 per share dividend.

The end of the accounting period for Luso Company is each December 31. Prepare the necessary journal entries for Luso Company to record these transactions using the space provided.

Luso Company - General Journal

Date	Debit	Credit

Computations:

Date	Debit	Credit

Computations:

Date	Debit	Credit

Computations:

Date	Debit	Credit

Computations:

Question Five

At the end of the accounting period, what is the carrying value of the Temporary Investment account for Luso Company from Question Four, above? Explain.

____

____

____

____

____

____

Answers to Self-Test for Chapter One

Answer to Question One

Cash. *The most liquid of all assets because no conversion is needed. We carry cash at its face value on the balance sheet.*

Temporary Investments. *An account used to invest idle cash for a short period of time; less than the operating cycle or one year whichever is longer.*

Accounts Receivable. *The sale has been made, we now await the cash. While many different terms of sale exist, commonly, businesses expect their customers to pay accounts within thirty days. Thus, receivables should be converted into cash within this time. However, not all credit sales will be repaid. Generally, the carrying value of receivables includes an allowance for doubtful accounts.*

Inventory. *The goods have been purchased, but not yet sold. The liquidity of inventory may be very different from one business to the next. It probably takes longer to make the sale than collect the cash from it so we list inventory after receivables.*

Prepaid Operating Costs and Other Receivables. *The prepaids include items such as prepaid insurance, rent, etc. Other Receivables are usually tied to investment revenue such as dividends or interest. Attempts should be made to insert prepaids and receivables into the current asset listing according to when they will be retired.*

While the above list is not exhaustive, it does contain the accounts most commonly used.

Answer to Question Two

The remaining 90 days represents the rest of the operating cycle. That is, it takes 90 days from the day the business buys its inventory to when it sells the inventory. For example, the average time a book will stay on the shelf and remain unsold is 90 days. Once sold, the customer takes 30 days to pay for it. Thus, the entire operating cycle, 90 + 30 = 120 days, is how long it takes before the business gets the cash "back" from clients that the business originally spent to buy the goods.

Answer to Question Three

Short-term or temporary investments are not defined by the particular investment securities chosen. Rather, the length of time the investment will be held determines whether it should be classified as a short-term investment. The nature of these investments dictates that cash is idle only temporarily and will be used in the not too distant future. Thus, when idle cash is invested for a long period of time it should not be classified as a short-term investment. In order to fit within the definition of a current asset, the holding period of a temporary investment cannot be longer than the greater of the operating cycle or one year.

Answer to Question Four

Luso Company - General Journal

Date October 1, 2014	Debit	Credit
Temporary Investment	33,000*	
Cash		33,000
To record the purchase of 1,000 shares of Mayhem Ltd. at $33 each.		

Computations:

1,000 x $33 = $33,000

Date November 11, 2014	Debit	Credit
Cash	9,000*	
Temporary Investment		9,900**
Realized Loss on Sale of Temporary Investment	900***	
To record a $900 loss on disposal of 300 shares of Mayhem Ltd., at $30 each.		

Computations:

*300 x $30 = $9,000
** 300 x $33 = $9,900
***$33 - $30 = $3 loss per share, 300 x $3 = $900 loss.

Date December 5, 2014	Debit	Credit
Dividend Revenue Receivable	546*	
Dividend Revenue		546
To record the $0.78 dividend declared on the 700 Mayhem Ltd. shares held.		

Computations:

*1,000 - 300 = 700 shares held
700 x $0.78 = $546

Date December 31, 2014	Debit	Credit
Unrealized Holding Loss on Temporary Investment	3,500*	
Temporary Investment		3,500
To record a $3,500 holding loss on 700 shares of Mayhem Ltd., at $28 each.		

Computations:

*$33 - $28 = $5 loss per share, 700 x $5 = $3,500 loss.

Answer to Question Five

On December 29, 2014 the Mayhem Ltd. shares are trading at their lowest price. Thus, the 700 shares held by Luso Company must reflect this price. Therefore, the carrying value of the Temporary Investment account will be: 700 x $28 = $19,600. We should verify this amount by posting the transactions to the ledger. Doing so would yield a T-account that looks like this:

Temporary Investment	
33,000	
	9,900
	3,500
19,600	

Practice Problems for Chapter One

Question One

On February 29, 2014, Sicily Company acquired 1,000 shares of common stock in each of three corporations at the following costs: Corporation A, $20,000; Corporation B, $10,000; and Corporation C, $30,000.

On September 3, 2014, Corporation C declared a $4.40 dividend per share. Sicily Company received the dividend check on October 5, 2014.

At the end of the annual accounting period, December 31, 2014, the quoted market prices per share were: Corporation A, $18; Corporation B, $8 and Corporation C, $31.

On January 17, 2015, Sicily Company sold all 3,000 shares of its investments in Corporations A, B and C. The selling prices per share were: Corporation A, $21; Corporation B, $7 and Corporation C, $32. Use the space provided to record all the journal entries required for Sicily Company's short-term investments.

Sicily Company - General Journal

Date	Debit	Credit

Computations:

Date	Debit	Credit

Computations:

Date	Debit	Credit

Computations:

Date	Debit	Credit

Computations:

Date	Debit	Credit

Date	Debit	Credit

Computations:

Date	Debit	Credit

Computations:

Date	Debit	Credit

Computations:

Date	Debit	Credit

Computations:

Date	Debit	Credit

Computations:

Question Two

Use the spaces provided below to post the journal entries from Question One, to Sicily Company's ledger. Describe how the temporary investments would be reported on the balance sheet and income statement at December 31, 2014 and December 31, 2015.

Sicily Company - General Journal

Cash

Temporary Investments (Corporation A)

Temporary Investments (Corporation B)

Temporary Investments (Corporation C)

Dividend Revenue Receivable

Dividend Revenue

Unrealized Holding Loss on Temporary Investments

Realized Gain on Sale of Temporary Investments

Realized Loss on Sale of Temporary Investments

Description of Financial Statements:

Solutions to Practice Problems for Chapter One

Solutions to Question One

Sicily Company - General Journal

Date February 29, 2014	**Debit**	**Credit**
Temporary Investments	20,000	
Cash		20,000
To record the purchase of 1,000 shares of Corporation A at $20 each.		

Computations:

**$20,000 ÷ 1,000 = $20 per share*

Date February 29, 2014	**Debit**	**Credit**
Temporary Investments	10,000	
Cash		10,000
To record the purchase of 1,000 shares of Corporation B at $10 each.		

Computations:

**$10,000 ÷ 1,000 = $10 per share*

Date February 29, 2014	**Debit**	**Credit**
Temporary Investments	30,000	
Cash		30,000
To record the purchase of 1,000 shares of Corporation C at $30 each.		

Computations:

**$30,000 ÷ 1,000 = $30 per share*

Date September 3, 2014	**Debit**	**Credit**
Dividend Revenue Receivable	4,400*	
Dividend Revenue		4,400
To record the $4.40 dividend per share declared on the 1,000 Corporation C shares held.		

Computations:

**1,000 x $4.40= $4,400*

Date October 5, 2014	*Debit*	*Credit*
Cash	*4,400*	
Dividend Revenue Receivable		*4,400*
To record payment of the $4.40 dividend per share declared on the 1,000 Corporation C shares held.		

Date December 31, 2014	*Debit*	*Credit*
Unrealized Holding Loss on Temporary Investments	*2,000**	
Temporary Investments		*2,000*
To record a $2,000 holding loss on 1,000 shares of Corporation A, now at $18 each.		

Computations:

**$20 - $18 = $2 loss per share, 1,000 x $2 = $2,000 loss.*

Date December 31, 2014	*Debit*	*Credit*
Unrealized Holding Loss on Temporary Investments	*2,000**	
Temporary Investments		*2,000*
To record a $2,000 holding loss on 1,000 shares of Corporation B, now at $8 each.		

Computations:

**$10 - $8 = $2 loss per share, 1,000 x $2 = $2,000 loss.*

Date January 17, 2015	*Debit*	*Credit*
Cash	*21,000**	
Temporary Investment		*18,000***
Realized Gain on Sale of Temporary Investments		*3,000****
To record a $3,000 gain on disposal of 1,000 shares of Corporation A., at $21 each.		

Computations:

**1,000 x $21 = $21,000*

*** carrying value on December 31, 2014*

****$21 - $18 = $3 gain per share, 1,000 x $3 = $3,000 gain.*

For your information: the $3,000 gain will not be used for tax purposes. Rather, $2,000 of the $3,000 gain is attributed to the unrealized holding loss taken on the December 31, 2014 income statement.

Date *January 17, 2015*	**Debit**	**Credit**
Cash	*7,000**	
Temporary Investment		*8,000***
Realized Loss on Sale of Temporary Investments	*1,000****	
To record a $1,000 loss on disposal of 1,000 shares of Corporation B, at $7 each.		

Computations:

**1,000 x $7 = $7,000*

***carrying value on December 31, 2014*

****$8 - $7 = $1 loss per share, 1,000 x $1 = $1,000 loss.*

Date *January 17, 2015*	**Debit**	**Credit**
Cash	*32,000**	
Temporary Investment		*30,000***
Realized Gain on Sale of Temporary Investments		*2,000****
To record a $2,000 gain on disposal of 1,000 shares of Corporation C, at $32 each.		

Computations:

**1,000 x $32 = $32,000*

***carrying value on December 31, 2014 (same as acquisition cost)*

****$32 - $30 = $2 gain per share, 1,000 x $2 = $2,000 gain.*

Solutions to Question Two

Your Company - General Journal

Cash

	20,000
	10,000
	30,000
4,400	
21,000	
7,000	
32,000	
4,400 (balance)	

Temporary Investments (Corporation A)

20,000	2,000
	18,000
0 (balance)	

Temporary Investments (Corporation B)

10,000	2,000
	8,000
0 (balance)	

Temporary Investments (Corporation C)

30,000	30,000
0 (balance)	

Dividend Revenue Receivable

4,400	4,400
0 (balance)	

Dividend Revenue

	4,400

Unrealized Holding Loss on Temporary Investments

2,000	
2,000	
4,000 (balance)	

Realized Gain on Sale of Temporary Investments

	3,000
	2,000
	5,000 (balance)

Realized Loss on Sale of Temporary Investments

1,000	

Note: Dividend revenue ($4,400) and the unrealized holding loss ($4,000) would be reported on the 2014 income statement. The realized gain ($5,000) and realized loss ($1,000) would be reported on the 2015 income statement. See also the discussion that follows.

Description of Financial Statements:

On December 31, 2014 the balance sheet would reflect $56,000 in Temporary Investments: $18,000 in Corporation A, $8,000 in Corporation B and $30,000 in Corporation C. At that time the Income

Statement would show $4,000 in unrealized holding losses. Together, these make up the $60,000 acquisition cost. In addition, there would be $4,400 in Dividend Revenues.

On December 31, 2015, the balance sheet would not show a Temporary Investments account as all the securities have been sold and the account would show a zero balance. However, the Income Statement would reflect the $5,000 in realized gains and $1,000 in realized losses. Recall that the income statement of the previous year showed $4,000 in unrealized losses.

Taking the two income statements together reflects what actually happened. Securities were purchased for $60,000 and sold for $60,000. The total losses (realized plus unrealized) amounted to $5,000, as did the gains. Thus, the cash account reflects the only reward from the short-term investments; $4,400 in dividend revenue.

Notes

Chapter Two - Carrying Inventory

The Reason for This Chapter

We classify inventory as a current asset because we expect it will be used up or sold within the upcoming year. Businesses that don't move their inventory won't be in business very long!

Does the price of inventory remain stable over time? Probably not. Think about the goods you buy in a department or grocery store. Do you expect to pay the same price this month as you did last? This year as last? Clearly, the answer is no.

As with temporary investments, we expect the dollar value of inventory to change over time. What value should we report? Determining the value of inventory represents a challenge for accountants. In this chapter we introduce two inventory systems and four methods of valuation.

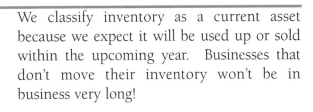

What Do You Already Know?

In this section of the chapter we ask you to complete a pre-test. It will get you thinking about what you already know about accounting. It will also serve as a link between what you learned in Chapter One and what you are about to learn in Chapter Two. After completing the pre-test, check your answers against the ones provided.

Pre-Test

Question One:

Place, in good order, the following accounts, as they should appear on the current asset section of the balance sheet:

Account Name	Description	Value ($)
Allowance for Doubtful Accounts	Estimated uncollectible receivables for the next 90 days.	5,540
Temporary Investments	Idle cash invested for 45 days.	6,570
Inventory	Average days before sale: 110	68,250
Cash	In bank accounts.	2,540
Accounts Receivable	Average time to collect: 90 days.	45,840
Prepaid Insurance	Policy is for 12 months.	4,600

Use the space provided below:

TOTAL CURRENT ASSETS	

Question Two:

The following prices were available for the shares of Space Unlimited Inc.:

Date	Price per Share
February 29, 2014	$45
March 31, 2014	$40
April 30 2014	$43

The management of Mallard Company purchased 150 shares of Space Unlimited on February 1, 2014 at $47 per share, for the purpose of investing idle cash for the next six months. Mallard Company ends its accounting period at the end of each month. Prepare the necessary journal entries to account for the temporary investment transaction, to date. Use the space provided:

Mallard Company - General Journal

Date	Debit	Credit

Computations:

Date	Debit	Credit

Computations:

Date	Debit	Credit

Computations:

Answers to Pre-Test

Answer to Question One

Cash		$2,540
Temporary Investments		6,570
Accounts Receivable	$45,840	
Less: Allowance for Doubtful Accounts	(5,540)	
Carrying value of Receivables		40,300
Inventory		68,250
Prepaid Insurance		4,600
TOTAL CURRENT ASSETS		$122,260

Mallard Company - General Journal

Date February 1, 2014	**Debit**	**Credit**
Temporary Investment	7,050*	
Cash		7,050
To record the purchase of 150 shares of Space Unlimited Inc. at $47 each		

Computations:

*150 x $47 = $7,050

Date February 29, 2014	**Debit**	**Credit**
Unrealized Holding Loss on Temporary Investment	300*	
Temporary Investment		300
To record the unrealized holding loss on 150 shares of Space Unlimited Inc. now valued at $45 each.		

Computations:

*150 x ($47 - $45) = $300

Date March 31, 2014	**Debit**	**Credit**
Unrealized Holding Loss on Temporary Investment	750*	
Temporary Investment		750
To record the unrealized holding loss on 150 shares of Space Unlimited Inc. now valued at $40 each.		

Computations:

*150 x ($45 - $40) = $750

As discussed in the previous chapter of this book no entry is made as at April 30, 2014 for the unrealized holding gain.

How This Chapter Relates to Chapters in This Book

Because inventory is a current asset account, we expect to liquidate it within the operating cycle or one year, whichever is longer. During that time we carry the inventory as a permanent balance sheet account. Accountants must report a dollar value for it at the end of each accounting period. This chapter demonstrates different systems and costing methods used to determine the carrying value of inventory.

Chapter One considered how to carry the value of Temporary Investments, a current asset account. Chapter Four will show us how to carry the value of longer-term or capital assets. Chapter Five classifies and carries specific liability and equity accounts. Chapters Three and Six provide a review in the form of practice cases.

What Are the Topics in This Chapter?

At what value should the business carry its inventory? Should the valuation method depend on the nature of the business? Do different methods really yield different results?

This chapter studies the carrying value of inventory. In it we examine the importance of selecting the appropriate method to account for inventory. We distinguish units from dollars. The reader should begin to understand how the choice of accounting method impacts the financial reports.

Two Inventory Systems

Topics Covered in Chapter Two	*Level of Importance*
Two Inventory Systems	
The Periodic System	***
The Perpetual System	**
Which System Should Be Used?	***

Topics Covered in Chapter Two	*Level of Importance*
The Need for Inventory Costing Methods	
Some Principles	***
When Costs Change	***
The Specific Identification Method	**
The Costing Problem	***
Alternative Costing Methods	**
First In, First Out (FIFO)	
Definition	***
Assumption	***
Costing with FIFO	***
Last In, First Out (LIFO)	
Definition	***
Assumption	***
Costing with LIFO	***
Weighted Average	
Definition	***
Assumption	***
Costing with Weighted Average	***
Comparing the Costing Methods	
Comparisons	**
Manipulations	**

Legend

*	indicates a low level of importance
**	indicates a medium level of importance
***	indicates a high level of importance

In Fundamentals of Accounting: Volume Two, Chapter Four used the periodic system of inventory management, extensively. For your convenience, this chapter opens with a brief review of the periodic system so we may contrast it with the perpetual system.

The Periodic System

In order to find the ending inventory balance, the periodic system requires a physical count of the inventory on hand. Once the ending inventory is known, we can calculate the cost of goods sold. In fact, its determination happens automatically through the income summary account.

At the end of each accounting period we close the temporary purchases account to income summary and replace the beginning inventory balance with the ending inventory balance. The net sum of these journal entries provides us with the costs of goods sold amount. No actual cost of goods sold account needs to exist. The cost of goods sold figure is a result of the closing entries at the end of the accounting period. Conceptually, it is easier to use a Cost of Goods Sold Schedule, as follows:

Beginning Merchandise Inventory (BI)	+	Purchases Of Merchandise (P)	=	Cost of Goods Available For Sale	–	Ending Merchandise Inventory (EI)	=	Cost of Goods Sold (CGS)

Try Learning Exercise One, to refresh your memory.

Now You Try It

Exercise One

You work in a greeting card shop. At the end of the last accounting period, a physical count showed there were 20,000 greeting cards in the shop. Let's assume the cost of all greeting cards remains at $1 (don't worry, the subject matter in this chapter will alter that unrealistic assumption). Thus, this accounting period began with $20,000 worth of merchandise inventory (20,000 cards x $1 each).

During this period, the shop purchased an additional $5,000 worth of cards. At the end of this period, the physical count showed

15,000 cards remained in the store. What is the amount of cost of goods sold that will be reported on the income statement for this accounting period?

Use the periodic inventory equation provided below:

Beginning Merchandise Inventory	+	Purchases Of Merchandise	=	Cost of Goods Available For Sale	–	Ending Merchandise Inventory	=	Cost of Goods Sold

Answers

Answer to Exercise One

Beginning Merchandise Inventory	+	Purchases Of Merchandise	=	Cost of Goods Available For Sale	–	Ending Merchandise Inventory	=	Cost of Goods Sold
$20,000	+	$5,000	=	$25,000	–	$15,000	=	$10,000

In this example we can see both the physical number of inventory units and its dollar cost. Why? We assumed that inventory always remained priced at $1. If the ending value of inventory is $15,000 there must be 15,000 units.

Assuming the cost of inventory never changes is unrealistic. Changing it is the primary focus of this chapter. Before doing so, we differentiate the periodic system from the perpetual system.

The Perpetual System

Use of the perpetual system necessitates computer support. Computer software keeps track of the inventory activity for each item. Journal entries are made directly to the Inventory and Cost

of Goods Sold accounts to monitor sales activity. Entries for the Inventory and Cash or Accounts Payable accounts are used to track purchases. Thus, the perpetual system keeps track of both cost of goods sold and ending inventory, at any time.

While the difference between the two systems may not seem significant, it is. The perpetual system provides instant information. At any time during the accounting period we know how many units have been sold and how many should be in storage. Under the periodic system, a physical count must be undertaken before either figure can be ascertained.

Under the perpetual system, a physical count facilitates inventory control. The computer can tell us how many units should be in stock, at any time. Should the actual inventory count be different, we know a problem exists. Events such as theft and spoilage reduce the number of units actually available for resale.

Let's use Learning Exercise Two to demonstrate how the journal entries for the two inventory systems differ:

Now you Try It

Exercise Two

Demonstrate which accounts are debited and credited for:

1. a sale of goods on credit
2. a purchase of goods for resale

when (a) a perpetual inventory system is used and (b) a periodic inventory system is used. Use the following provided space:

We record a sale of goods, when the perpetual system is used, as follows:

Date	Debit	Credit

Date	Debit	Credit

And when a periodic system is used:

Date	Debit	Credit

A purchase of goods for resale, when the perpetual system is used, is recorded as follows:

Date	Debit	Credit

And when the periodic system is used:

Date	Debit	Credit

Answers

Answer to Exercise Two

We record a sale of goods, when the perpetual system is used, as follows:

Date	***Debit***	***Credit***
Accounts Receivable	*XXX*	
Sales Revenue		*XXX*

Date	***Debit***	***Credit***
Cost of Goods Sold	*YYY*	
Inventory		*YYY*

And when the periodic inventory system is used:

Date	***Debit***	***Credit***
Accounts Receivable	*XXX*	
Sales Revenue		*XXX*

Note that there is no entry at this point to record cost of goods sold under the periodic system.

A purchase of goods for resale, when the perpetual system is used, is recorded as follows:

Date	***Debit***	***Credit***
Inventory	*AAA*	
Cash (or Accounts Payable)		*AAA*

And when the periodic system is used:

Date	*Debit*	*Credit*
Purchases	AAA	
Cash (or Accounts Payable)		AAA

Now, let's revisit the greeting card example to further demonstrate how the two inventory systems differ.

Now You Try It

Exercise Three

You work in a greeting card shop. The computer software used in this business keeps track of each card as it is sold. At the beginning of the accounting period, records showed there were 20,000 greeting cards in the shop. Let's keep the assumption that all greeting cards cost $1. Thus, the beginning inventory value is $20,000.

During this period, the shop purchased an additional $5,000 worth of cards. At the end of this period, the computer records show 10,000 cards were sold. What inventory value should be reported on the balance sheet at the end of this accounting period?

The computer software has recorded all the journal entries for you. We will not show them here. Show us what the Inventory and Cost of Goods Sold T-accounts would look like for the month. Show the balances in the space provided below:

Answers

Answer to Exercise Three

Inventory	
$20,000 (beginning)	
$5,000 (purchased)	
	$10,000 (sold)
Bal. $15,000 (ending)	

Cost of Goods Sold	
$10,000	

How is this different from the periodic system used in Learning Exercise One? Here, we can complete the financial reports without performing a physical count of the inventory. Cost of Goods Sold is tracked with each sales activity in its own account. As well, the inventory account tracks the inventory activity (in and out). Although this example has been simplified because the month's totals were posted instead of the individual transactions, the message should still be clear. The perpetual system provides both the ending inventory and cost of goods sold values without taking a physical count or completing a schedule. Of course, it uses computer systems to facilitate the record keeping.

Which System Should Be Used?

The ***periodic*** inventory system is the less sophisticated of the two. It requires a physical count of the inventory at the end of the period. It is appropriate when the cost of computerized systems can not be justified. The main disadvantage of this method is the lack of control it offers over theft and spoilage. For example, items stolen are often assumed to simply have been sold.

The periodic system uses the Cost of Goods Sold schedule, as this number is difficult to ascertain by simply looking at the journal entries. During an accounting period, the total of all purchases and sales are recorded. At the end of the period the remaining units on hand are physically counted. The ending value of the prior period becomes the beginning inventory of the next period.

The ***perpetual*** system involves more clerical effort, but offers much better control over inventory when it functions effectively and efficiently. A separate record is kept for each type of inventory. These records are updated on a transaction by transaction basis. Should a physical count be undertaken, the records will show exactly how much inventory should be in stock. It becomes easy to deduce if items are being lost or stolen. In practice, it is important to conduct a physical count from time to time to test the accuracy of the results provided by the perpetual system.

The use of the perpetual system has greatly increased with the advances made in technology. Most stores now use a computerized inventory system that is tied directly to store cash registers. This reduces costs and increases the convenience of using a perpetual inventory system.

The basic differences between the periodic and perpetual inventory systems are described in the table below:

Account	Periodic	Perpetual
Inventory	Not changed during the period. Purchases are recorded in the Purchases account then closed to Income Summary. Ending Inventory replaces Beginning Inventory after the physical count.	Inventory account is increased and decreased for each purchase and sale during the accounting period. No purchases account exists.
Cost of Goods Sold	Only determined at the end of the period by using the Cost of Goods Sold Schedule BI + P - EI = CGS. (Some businesses use a Cost of Goods Sold account in a periodic system, but this approach is not discussed in this course.)	Is recorded at the time of each sale into a Cost of Goods Sold account. Allows for a direct measure of cost of goods sold anytime during the period.

The choice depends largely on the importance of having timely information versus the cost of implementing computerized systems. For simplicity, we use the periodic system to demonstrate alternative costing methods in this chapter.

The Need for Inventory Costing Methods

Some Principles

We determine the value of inventory held by the business according to its historical cost. Any expenditures related to the purchase of inventory, such as transportation, duty, non-recoverable sales taxes, will be included in the cost of the inventory. This is an application of the cost principle.

The matching principle dictates that any costs incurred in generating revenues should be matched to and reported at the same time as those revenues. Thus, when an inventory unit is sold its cost should be reported during the same accounting period as the sale. If the cost of an inventory item never changes, the matching process is simple. As depicted in Learning Exercises One and Three, items moving in and out of inventory were all at the same cost. There was no costing issue. Units could be interchanged with dollars. Unfortunately, this does not represent reality. The cost of inventory changes all the time. This creates a need for alternative Inventory Costing Methods.

When Costs Change

Changing costs complicates the matching process. It becomes desirable to physically match each inventory unit sold with its original cost. In order to do this, the accounting system must physically track each unit from purchase to sale in order to make the match. Sometimes this is possible. And sometimes it is easy. For example, if automobile number #WX7863001 is sold, we know its original cost if an individual inventory record was kept for unit #WX7863001. We can specifically identify the unit being sold.

We cover the first inventory costing method, Specific Identification, next.

The Specific Identification Method

This inventory costing method physically tracks each item from purchase to sale. We refer to this as the cost flow assumption. In order to trace the units, some kind of identification label must exist for each item, along with an inventory record.

Now You Try It

Exercise Four

The Central Supply Company has in inventory on May 1, three units of item K, all purchased on the same date at a price of $600 per unit. During the month, the following activities took place:

Date	Explanation	Units	Unit Cost	Tag Number
May 1	Inventory	3	$600	515, 516, 517
May 3	Purchase	2	$650	518,519
May 12	Sale	3		515, 518, 519
May 19	Purchase	2	$760	520, 521
May 25	Sale	1		516

The month end physical count revealed 3 units left in inventory. Compute the cost of goods sold and ending inventory using the specific identification cost flow assumption and periodic inventory system. For convenience, use the table provided on the next page:

Beginning Merchandise Inventory (Item K)	+	Purchases Of Merchandise (Item K)	=	Cost of Goods Available For Sale (Item K)	–	Ending Merchandise Inventory (Item K)	=	Cost of Goods Sold (Item K)
	+		=		–		=	

Answers

Answer to Exercise Four

Under the periodic system, the calendar dates of individual activity within the accounting period are not important. However, under the specific identification system each piece of inventory must be individually traced. This is possible because we have a unique tag or label number for each unit of Item K. We must use a tracking system, as follows:

Beginning Merchandise Inventory (Item K)	+	Purchases Of Merchandise (Item K)	=	Cost of Goods Available For Sale (Item K)	–	Ending Merchandise Inventory (Item K)	=	Cost of Goods Sold (Item K)
		518 @ $650						515 @ $600
515 @ $600		519 @ $650				517 @ $600		518 @ $650
516 @ $600		520 @ $760				520 @ $760		519 @ $650
517 @ $600		521 @ $760				521 @ $760		516 @ $600
$1,800	+	$2,820	=	$4,620	–	$2,120	=	$2,500

During the month, the actual units sold of item K are tag numbers 515, 518, 519 and 516. Therefore, we could quickly calculate the cost of goods sold as:

(2 x $600) + (2 x $650) = $2,500

However, we must still track the goods to determine the ending inventory value. Remember, the periodic system requires a physical count of the warehoused goods at the end of the period.

Whether a periodic or perpetual system is used, the Specific Identification inventory costing method requires tracking of each individual inventory unit, for each item type. We have created a Cost of Goods Sold Schedule for item K, in which we also traced the activity of each item K unit.

The Costing Problem

If the cost of inventory items never changed, then valuing inventory would be relatively simple. Remember how easy this was for the card shop in Learning Exercises One and Three. Every card cost $1. If it were possible to trace each inventory item from its purchase to sale, then the matching principle would be satisfied. Again, costing the inventory would be simple, as each unit would be specifically identified.

In many cases it is extremely costly to track each unit. In some cases it is not even possible. The Specific Identification method is impractical whenever new items are mixed with old ones. Consider the following example:

Each time a box of nails is purchased, its contents are emptied into a large barrel. The nails are offered for re-sale as a bulk item. That is, the shopper simply grabs as many nails as needed and throws them into a bag. The price charged for a bag of nails is by weight. Thus, each nail loses its identity. A physical match cannot be made between each nail sold and its purchase cost.

The Cost Flow Assumption

Accounting traces cost flows, not the physical flow of goods. When units can be specifically identified and traced, the two flows are the same. When units cannot be tracked, we have a costing problem.

Costing problems arise when: 1) the purchase price on an item varies and 2) no specific identification is possible. When the costing problem exists, accountants must make a cost flow assumption about the movement of inventory. This affects the financial statements in two possible ways: the Ending Inventory on the balance sheet and the Cost of Goods Sold on the income statement each differ depending on the cost flow assumption chosen.

While the matching principle should be upheld, only the Specific Identification method permits a "true" match. The alternative costing methods each have a different influence on inventory valuation. They differ with respect to allocating value between ending inventory and cost of goods sold.

Alternative Costing Methods

The selection of an inventory costing method should be rational and systematic. Within the same business, different methods may be used to value different inventory items. However, the reasoning behind the choice of a method should be sound. That is, the cost flow assumption selected should reflect how the inventory is used.

Different costing methods impact the financial statements differently. Accountants must disclose a note about the selected costing method. This disclosure helps the users of accounting information understand and determine the implications of the selected policy.

We examine three alternative costing methods, each with a different cost flow assumption, next. They are FIFO, LIFO and Weighted Average.

First In, First Out (FIFO)

Definition

Companies usually meet business demands by using the older units in inventory first. First In, First Out. This physical flow of inventory is probably the most common. That is, the oldest units in inventory are usually sold before the newer ones.

Assumption

Since our concern is with the cost flow, we use a costing method that best matches the physical flow of the goods. Under the FIFO approach, we use the oldest purchase prices available to cost the units sold during the accounting period. This makes sense. If we assume that the oldest units are sold first, then the oldest prices reflect the cost of goods sold for that period.

Costing with FIFO

Now You Try It

Exercise Five

Let's revisit the Central Supply Company. Now assume the company generally sells the oldest units in inventory first. On May 1, it has three units of item K in inventory. Each was purchased at a price of $600. During the month, the following activities took place:

Date	Explanation	Units	Unit Cost	Tag Number
May 1	Inventory	3	$600	Unknown
May 3	Purchase	2	$650	Unknown
May 12	Sale	3		Unknown
May 19	Purchase	2	$760	Unknown
May 25	Sale	1		Unknown

At the end of the month a physical count revealed 3 units were left in inventory. Compute the cost of goods sold and ending inventory using the FIFO cost flow assumption and periodic inventory system. For convenience, use the table provided:

Beginning Merchandise Inventory (Item K)	+	Purchases Of Merchandise (Item K)	=	Cost of Goods Available For Sale (Item K)	–	Ending Merchandise Inventory (Item K)	=	Cost of Goods Sold (Item K)
	+		=		–		=	

Answers

Answer to Exercise Five

Beginning Merchandise Inventory (Item K)	+	Purchases Of Merchandise (Item K)	=	Cost of Goods Available For Sale (Item K)	–	Ending Merchandise Inventory (Item K)	=	Cost of Goods Sold (Item K)
3 x $600 = $1,800	+	(2 x $650) + (2 x $760) = $2,820	=	$4,620	–	(2 x $760) = (1 x $650) = $2,170	=	$2,450

**Under FIFO it is assumed the oldest units were sold first. Therefore the newest units must be in ending inventory.*

FIFO is probably the most common costing method as it reflects the usual physical flow of goods from purchase to sale. However, it does not mean the FIFO approach should always be selected. Other costing methods may provide a better match between costs and revenues. Consider LIFO, next.

Last In, First Out (LIFO)

Definition

Companies sometimes meet business demands by selecting the newer inventory units to be used first. In this situation, the physical flow of inventory is normally on a last in, first out basis. That is, the newest units in inventory are sold before the older ones.

Assumption

As our concern is with cost flow, we use a costing method that best matches the physical flow of the goods. Under the LIFO approach, we use the newest purchase prices available to cost the units sold during this accounting period. This makes sense. If the newest units are sold first, then newest prices must reflect the cost of the goods sold this period.

Costing with LIFO

Now You Try It

Exercise Six.

Let's revisit the Central Supply Company. Assume the company sells the newest units in inventory, first. On May 1, it has three units of item K in its inventory. Each unit cost $600. During the month, the following activities took place:

Date	Explanation	Units	Unit Cost	Tag Number
May 1	Inventory	3	$600	Unknown
May 3	Purchase	2	$650	Unknown
May 12	Purchase	2	$760	Unknown
May 19	Sale	3		Unknown
May 25	Sale	1		Unknown

At the end of the month a physical count revealed 3 units were left in inventory. Compute the cost of goods sold and ending inventory using the LIFO cost flow assumption and periodic inventory system. For convenience, use the table provided below:

Beginning Merchandise Inventory (Item K)	+	Purchases Of Merchandise (Item K)	=	Cost of Goods Available For Sale (Item K)	–	Ending Merchandise Inventory (Item K)	=	Cost of Goods Sold (Item K)
	+		=		–		=	

Answers

Answer to Exercise Six

Beginning Merchandise Inventory (Item K)	+	Purchases Of Merchandise (Item K)	=	Cost of Goods Available For Sale (Item K)	–	Ending Merchandise Inventory (Item K)	=	Cost of Goods Sold (Item K)
3 x $600 = $1,800	+	(2 x $650) + (2 x $760) = $2,820	=	$4,620	–	3 x $600 = $1,800	=	$2,820

*Under LIFO it is assumed the newest units were sold first. Therefore the oldest units must be in ending inventory.

Weighted Average

Definition

Companies sometimes meet business demands by using any inventory. In this situation, the physical flow of inventory is indeterminable. Therefore, it is appropriate that when a unit is sold, the weighted average cost is used to determine the cost of goods sold.

Assumption

We always seek to use a costing method that best matches the physical flow of the goods. Under the Weighted Average approach, we spread the total cost of purchases across all units, equally. We must calculate the weighted average cost per unit to do so. This approach brings results that fall between LIFO and FIFO. However, when inventory is moved out rapidly, the weighted average results are closest to FIFO.

Costing with Weighted Average

Now You Try It

Exercise Seven

Our last visit to the Central Supply Company. Finally, assume the company uses the weighted average cost of goods sold to value inventory. On May 1, it has three units of item K in inventory. Each cost $600. During the month, the following activities took place:

Date	Explanation	Units	Unit Cost	Tag Number
May 1	Inventory	3	$600	Unknown
May 3	Purchase	2	$650	Unknown
May 12	Sale	3		Unknown
May 19	Purchase	2	$760	Unknown
May 25	Sale	1		Unknown

At the end of the month a physical count revealed 3 units were left in inventory. Compute the cost of goods sold and ending inventory using the weighted average cost flow assumption and periodic inventory system.

We calculate the weighted average cost per unit as: Cost of Goods Available for Sale ÷ Number of Units Available for Sale

Beginning Merchandise Inventory (Item K)		Purchases Of Merchandise (Item K)		Cost of Goods Available For Sale (Item K)		Ending Merchandise Inventory (Item K)		Cost of Goods Sold (Item K)
	+		=		–		=	

Answers

Answer to Exercise Seven

We calculate the weighted average cost as: $4,620 ÷ 7 = $660

Beginning Merchandise Inventory (Item K)		Purchases Of Merchandise (Item K)		Cost of Goods Available For Sale (Item K)		Ending Merchandise Inventory (Item K)		Cost of Goods Sold (Item K)
3 x $600 = $1,800	+	(2 x $650) + (2 x $760) = $2,820	=	$4,620	–	3 x $660 = $1,980	=	$2,640

*Under Weighted Average the weighted average cost is used to value units in ending inventory.

Comparing the Costing Methods

Comparisons

In Learning Exercises Four, Five, Six and Seven, we used Central Supply Company and four different costing methods to calculate ending inventory and cost of goods sold. We will summarize these results in a table.

First, let's assume the selling price of the four units sold during the month of May was $900 each. Therefore, regardless of the costing method used, the Sales Revenue for May will be $900 x 4 = $3,600.

Next, we will compute the Gross Profit for each method. Recall, Gross Profit is the difference between Sales Revenue and Cost of Goods Sold. Gross profit represents the profit from selling merchandise inventory before any other operating costs are considered.

Last, we ask you to confirm the pattern of prices. For Central Supply Company, during the month of May, the price of Item K was rising. Recall the May 1, cost per unit was $600, on May 3 that price rose to $650 and by May 19 it was $760 per unit.

The differences between each costing method, given rising prices, can be shown as:

	Income Statement Accounts			Balance Sheet
Method	**Sales Revenue ($)**	**Cost of Goods Sold ($)**	**Gross Profit ($)**	**Ending Inventory ($)**
Specific Identification	3,600	2,500	1,100	2,120
FIFO	3,600	2,450	1,150	2,170
LIFO	3,600	2,820	780	1,800
Weighted Average	3,600	2,640	960	1,980

The Specific Identification costing method provides the truest result, if no manipulation has taken place. Remember, it is not always possible, or cost-effective to use this method. We discuss its pitfalls in the next section.

The remaining techniques all make assumptions about the appropriate pattern of costs:

In a period of rising prices LIFO yields the highest cost of goods sold and lowest gross profit because it uses the latest (and highest) price to report income statement activity. Therefore the older (and lowest) prices are reflected on the balance sheet.

In a period of rising prices FIFO yields the opposite result. Because the cost of Item K is rising, FIFO gives the lowest cost of goods sold and highest gross profit; FIFO uses the oldest (and lowest) price to report income statement activity. Therefore the newer (and highest) prices are reflected on the balance sheet.

The Weighted Average result falls between LIFO and FIFO. This makes sense. Because the cost of Item K is rising, FIFO gives the lowest cost of goods sold and highest gross profit. LIFO gives the highest cost of goods sold and lowest gross profit. Weighted Average uses the average price, which falls in between the highest and lowest. The weighted average price is also reflected on the balance sheet.

When costs are falling, the LIFO and FIFO results switch. Gross Profit will be higher under LIFO and lower under FIFO. The Weighted Average results tend to stay in between. Mixed cost patterns yield mixed results.

Two costing methods are particularly vulnerable to manipulation by management. We consider each, next.

Manipulations

Use of the Specific Identification and LIFO costing methods may lead to manipulations by management. Sometimes they are thought to be less desirable than other methods, as the users of financial statements may suspect these reports represent a distorted view of reality.

Specific Identification

Management might "pick and choose" items to be sold based on their cost, especially if the items in question are identical, or nearly identical. By doing so they influence the cost of goods sold. If you choose to sell the cheaper units during an accounting period, your cost of goods sold will be lower and hence your income higher, for that period. The opposite is also true.

LIFO

Consider the following scenario: a company purchases goods at the end of the accounting period when prices have fallen. Cost of goods sold, reflecting the newest cheaper price, is low. Thus, income will be high. The income statement will reflect the price of the new goods, even though these goods were not sold during the period.

Alternatively, management may elect to use LIFO when the cost of goods are rising. Under this circumstance the LIFO costing method causes the cost of goods sold to be high, lowering taxable income. The government frowns on such manipulations as their revenues from taxation would be less. In Canada, the use of LIFO is generally not permitted for tax purposes.

Weighted Average cannot be manipulated per se, but calculations can result in a rounding error.

What You Have Learned in This Chapter

The firm decides whether it will use a periodic or perpetual inventory system to determine the value of ending inventory value and cost of goods sold. The periodic method requires a physical count, at the end of the accounting period, to determine the actual number of units in ending inventory. Record keeping for this system is relatively simple as no Cost of Goods Sold account need exist. We may use a Cost of Goods Sold Schedule for convenience, but the cost of goods sold amount can actually be determined as a by-product of the closing journal entries.

The perpetual system offers better control over inventory as both the cost of goods sold and inventory value may be ascertained anytime during the accounting period. A Cost of Goods Sold account, used in conjunction with the Inventory account, keeps track of daily activity. Computerized systems are usually required to handle the management of inventory.

When the cost of goods changes, a costing problem arises. A cost flow assumption must be made in order to select an appropriate costing method. Four techniques were examined in this chapter: Specific Identification, FIFO, LIFO and Weighted Average. Each assumes a different cost flow for the inventory item under evaluation. Companies may use more than one method for different inventory items. Management, with the help of accountants, must justify its costing method and disclose it in a note on the financial statements.

Reviewing the section "Important Terms in this Chapter" provides a great summary. It also serves to test your understanding. If you can define all these terms, you most likely have a good grasp of the topics covered. You will further test this knowledge by completing the Self-Test and Practice Problems. Good Luck.

Important Terms in This Chapter

Cost Flow Assumption: is generally based on an approximation of the physical flow of goods through the inventory system, from purchase to sale. Used to determine the appropriate costing method.

FIFO (First In, First Out): this inventory costing method assumes the oldest goods in inventory are used up (sold) first.

Gross Profit: the difference between sales revenue and cost of goods sold. It is the profit from selling merchandise before other operating expenses are considered. Also known as Gross Margin.

Inventory Costing Method: there are four; Specific Identification, FIFO, LIFO and Weighted Average.

LIFO (Last In, First Out): this costing method assumes the newest goods in inventory are used up first.

Periodic Inventory System: no cost of goods sold account needs to exist. A physical count at the end of the period provides the ending inventory value. Cost of goods sold can be determined through the Income Summary account (closing process), or by the use of a cost of goods sold schedule at the end of the period.

Perpetual Inventory System: the Cost of Goods Sold account is debited and the Inventory account is credited for the cost of each item sold. Both amounts are known instantly. Generally requires computer support.

Specific Identification: a costing method that tracks each inventory unit from its purchase to sale. In order to use this method we must be able to specifically identify each unit and its cost when it is sold.

Weighted Average: this costing method spreads the total cost of units available for sale equally across all units.

Should You Move on to the Next Chapter?

It's time to check and see if you are comfortable with your new knowledge. Complete the Self-Test and Practice Problems to determine whether or not you are ready to move on to the next Chapter.

Self-Test for Chapter Two

Question One

When a perpetual inventory system is used, the cost of goods sold for the period is known at the date of each sale. In contrast, when a periodic inventory system is used, cost of goods sold for the period cannot be known until the end of the accounting period. Explain why these statements are correct.

Question Two

Critique each of the following two statements:

The inventory account on the balance sheet and cost of goods sold on the income statement are determined independently.

Different inventory costing methods will lead to the same result.

Question Three

On September 3, 2014, Slyster Inc. sold 3,000 units of inventory at a price of $1.50 each, on credit. On September 5, 2014, it replaced the sold inventory by ordering 4,000 units on account. The goods were shipped and the invoice received on September 5, 2014. The cost of these units has remained stable, at a price of $0.75 each, for the past year.

Prepare the necessary journal entries for September 3 and September 5, 2014 assuming Slyster Inc. uses, 1) the perpetual system, and 2) the periodic system. Use the space provided below:

Date	Debit	Credit

Computations

Date	Debit	Credit

Computations

Date	Debit	Credit

Computations

Date	Debit	Credit

Date	Debit	Credit

Computations

Date	Debit	Credit

Question Four

The following data was taken from the records of Two Sisters Ltd. at December 31, 2014:

Sales revenue	$120,000
Administrative expense	$10,000
Selling expense	$ 20,000
Income tax rate	25%
Gross profit	$48,000

Required:

Calculate and insert the missing amounts for the company's income statement :

Two Sisters Ltd.
Income Statement
For the year ending, __________

Sales revenue		$120,000
Cost of goods sold		____
Gross profit		
Operating expenses:		
administrative expense	$10,000	
selling expense	20,000	
Total operating expenses		____
Pretax income		
Income tax expense (25%)		____
Net income		====

Answers to Self-Test for Chapter Two

Answer to Question One

Under the perpetual inventory system two things happen at the date of each sale: (1) the units sold and their costs are removed from the perpetual inventory record and the new inventory balance is determined; (2) the cost of goods sold is determined from the perpetual inventory record and an entry is made as a debit to cost of goods sold and a credit to inventory.

In contrast, the periodic system is such that the cost of goods sold for each sale is not known at the time of sale. At the end of the period, cost of goods sold can be determined by adding the beginning inventory amount to the total cost of goods purchased for the period and subtracting from that total the ending inventory amount (BI + P - EI - CGS). The ending inventory amount must be determined by means of a physical inventory count of the goods remaining on hand.

Answer to Question Two

a) In fact, the opposite is true. We split the total inventory value (cost of goods available for sale) between ending inventory and the cost of goods sold. The balance sheet captures what is left at the end of the period. The income statement measures costs incurred during the period. Any cost not captured on the income statement must be reflected on the balance sheet, and vice versa. Therefore, the two financial statements are directly related in determining inventory value.

b) When the costs of goods are changing, different inventory costing methods will yield different results. This is the central dilemma surrounding the topics "the Costing Problem" and "Alternative Costing Methods", in this chapter. Management, with the help of accountants, must use judgement in determining which method is most suitable for select inventory items. Management must also disclose the reasons for the choice of costing method. This allows readers of financial statements to judge if the valuation method is appropriate. They may want to compare results with other companies. If costs never changed, the four inventory costing methods would yield the same results. This situation is highly improbable.

Answer to Question Three

As the cost of each unit has remained stable at $0.75, for the past year, no costing problem exits. We record Slyster Inc.'s sale of goods, when the perpetual system is used, as follows:

Date September 3, 2014	**Debit**	**Credit**
Accounts Receivable	$4,500	
Sales Revenue		$4,500
To record the sale of 3,000 units on account at $1.50 each.		

Computations

3,000 x $1.50 = $4,500

Date September 3, 2014	**Debit**	**Credit**
Cost of Goods Sold	$2,250	
Inventory		$2,250
To record the use of 3,000 units to satisfy a sale, at a cost of $0.75 each.		

Computations

3,000 x $0.75 = $2,250

Under the periodic inventory system only the sale is recorded, before a physical count is made:

Date September 3, 2014	**Debit**	**Credit**
Accounts Receivable	$4,500	
Sales Revenue		$4,500
To record the sale of 3,000 units on account at $1.50 each.		

We debit the Inventory account to record the purchase of goods for sale, when the perpetual system is used:

Date September 5, 2014	**Debit**	**Credit**
Inventory	3,000	
Accounts Payable		3,000
To record the purchase of 4,000 units on account at $0.75 each.		

Computations

4,000 x $0.75 = $3,000

And when a periodic system is used, we debit the Purchase account:

Date September 5, 2014	**Debit**	**Credit**
Purchases	3,000	
Accounts Payable		3,000
To record the purchase of 4,000 units on account at $0.75 each.		

Answer to Question Four

The missing information appears in bold. The computations are shown at the end of the answer.

Two Sisters Ltd.
Income Statement
For the year ending, December 31, 2014

Sales revenue		$120,000
Cost of goods sold		**72,000**
Gross profit		48,000
Operating expenses:		
administrative expense	$10,000	
selling expense	20,000	
Total operating expenses		**30,000**
Pretax income		**18,000**
Income tax expense (25%)		**4,500**
Net income		**$13,500**

Computations:
$120,000 - $48,000 = $72,000
$10,000 + $20,000 = $30,000
$48,000 - $30,000 = $18,000
$18,000 x 25% = $4,500
$18,000 - $4,500 = $13,500

Practice Problems for Chapter Two

Question One

Lake Limited buys pool accessories and water toys for resale. One of its most popular items, a water mattress, sells at a price of $40 each. Transactions involving this item during the month of June 2014, are as follows:

Date	Explanation	Units	Unit Cost	Tag Number
June 1	Inventory	50	$20	unknown
June 3	Purchase	200	$18	unknown
June 12	Sale	200		unknown
June 19	Purchase	300	$16	unknown
June 25	Sale	100		unknown

At the end of June, a physical count revealed 250 water mattresses were left in inventory. The company uses the periodic system to account for inventory.

Required:
Compute the cost of goods sold and ending inventory using the LIFO, Weighted Average and FIFO costing methods. Make a comment about the cost flow assumption for each. For convenience, you should complete the tables provided below:

Beginning Merchandise Inventory (Water Mattress)	+	Purchases Of Merchandise (Water Mattress)	=	Cost of Goods Available For Sale (Water Mattress)	–	Ending Merchandise Inventory (Water Mattress)	=	Cost of Goods Sold (Water Mattress)
	+		=		–		=	

Comment:

Weighted average unit price = Cost of Goods Available for Sale ÷ Number of Units Available for Sale.

Beginning Merchandise Inventory (Water Mattress)	+	Purchases Of Merchandise (Water Mattress)	=	Cost of Goods Available For Sale (Water Mattress)	–	Ending Merchandise Inventory (Water Mattress)	=	Cost of Goods Sold (Water Mattress)
	+		=		–		=	

Comment:

____

____

____

____

Beginning Merchandise Inventory (Water Mattress)	+	Purchases Of Merchandise (Water Mattress)	=	Cost of Goods Available For Sale (Water Mattress)	–	Ending Merchandise Inventory (Water Mattress)	=	Cost of Goods Sold (Water Mattress)
	+		=		–		=	

Comment:

____

____

____

____

Question Two

Use the information computed in Question One to complete the table below for Lake Limited. Compare the results for each costing method. Explain your findings in the comments section, following the table.

	Income Statement Accounts			Balance Sheet
Method	**Sales Revenue ($)**	**Cost of Goods Sold ($)**	**Gross Profit ($)**	**Ending Inventory ($)**
LIFO				
Weighted Average				
FIFO				

Comment:

____

____

____

____

Question Three

The records at the end of January 2015 for Sistars Company showed the following activity for Item A:

Date	Transaction	Units	Total Cost	Identification number
December 31, 2014	Inventory	1	$166	AA
January 9, 2015	Purchase	2	$375	AB,AC
January 11, 2015	Sale (at $450 per unit)	2		AA,AB
January 20, 2015	Purchase	5	$800	AD,AE, AF, AG, AH
January 27, 2015	Sale (at $440 per unit)	3		AD,AE,AF

Required:
The company uses a periodic system and the Specific Identification costing model. Complete the table provided below, for January 2015:

Beginning Merchandise Inventory (Item A)	+	Purchases Of Merchandise (Item A)	=	Cost of Goods Available For Sale (Item A)	–	Ending Merchandise Inventory (Item A)	=	Cost of Goods Sold (Item A)
	+		=		–		=	

Computations:

Has management manipulated inventory costing to its benefit? Explain.

____

____

____

____

____

____

Solutions to Practice Problems for Chapter Two

Solutions to Question One

Using the LIFO costing method:

Beginning Merchandise Inventory (Water Mattress)	+	Purchases Of Merchandise (Water Mattress)	=	Cost of Goods Available For Sale (Water Mattress)	–	Ending Merchandise Inventory (Water Mattress)	=	Cost of Goods Sold (Water Mattress)
50 x $20 = $1,000	+	(200 x $18) + (300 x $16) = $8,400	=	$9,400	–	(50 x $20) + (200 x $18) = $4,600	=	$4,800

Comment: *Under the LIFO cost flow assumption it is assumed that the newest units were sold first. Thus the 250 mattresses remaining in inventory are the oldest units.*

Using the Weighted Average costing method:

We calculate the weighted average cost as: $9,400 ÷ 550 = $17.09 (rounded)

Beginning Merchandise Inventory (Water Mattress)	+	Purchases Of Merchandise (Water Mattress)	=	Cost of Goods Available For Sale (Water Mattress)	–	Ending Merchandise Inventory (Water Mattress)	=	Cost of Goods Sold (Water Mattress)
50 x $20 = $1,000	+	(200 x $18) + (300 x $16) = $8,400	=	$9,400	–	250 x $17.09 = $4,273	=	$5,127

Comment: *Under the weighted average cost flow assumption, the total cost of units available for sale is spread equally across all units. Therefore, the weighted average cost per unit is used to value the 250 units remaining in inventory.*

Using the FIFO costing method:

Beginning Merchandise Inventory (Water Mattress)		Purchases Of Merchandise (Water Mattress)		Cost of Goods Available For Sale (Water Mattress)		Ending Merchandise Inventory (Water Mattress)		Cost of Goods Sold (Water Mattress)
	+		=		–		=	
50 x \$20 = \$1,000	+	(200 x \$18) + (300 x \$16) = \$8,400	=	\$9,400	–	(250 x \$16) = \$4,000	=	\$5,400

Comment: *Under the FIFO cost flow assumption it is assumed that the oldest units were sold first. Thus the 250 mattresses remaining in inventory are the newest units.*

Solutions to Question Two

	Income Statement Accounts			Balance Sheet
Method	**Sales Revenue (\$)**	**Cost of Goods Sold (\$)**	**Gross Profit (\$)**	**Ending Inventory (\$)**
LIFO	12,000	4,800	7,200	4,600
Weighted Average	12,000	5,127	6,873	4,273
FIFO	12,000	5,400	6,600	4,000

First we compute the sales revenue as \$12,000 (300 x \$40). It is the same for each costing method. Next we compute the Gross Profit for each costing method by deducting the Cost of Goods Sold from the Sales Revenue.

You should note that costs were falling over the entire period.

Use of FIFO yields the highest cost of goods sold and lowest gross profit because it uses the oldest (and highest) price to report income statement activity. Therefore the newer (and lowest) prices are reflected on the balance sheet, yielding the smallest ending inventory value.

Use of LIFO yields the opposite result. Because the cost of the water mattresses is falling, LIFO gives the lowest cost of goods sold and highest gross profit. It uses the newest (and lowest) price to report income statement activity. Therefore the oldest (and highest) prices are reflected on the balance sheet, yielding the largest ending inventory value.

Use of the Weighted Average method provides results that fall between LIFO and FIFO. This makes sense. Because the cost of the water mattresses is falling, LIFO shows the lowest cost of goods sold and highest gross profit, whereas FIFO shows the highest cost of goods sold and lowest gross profit (as discussed above). Weighted Average uses the average price, which lies somewhere between the highest and lowest price. The weighted average price is also reflected on the balance sheet.

This example portrays opposite results to those found in the "Comparing the Costing Methods" section of this chapter. There, the prices were rising.

Solutions to Question Three

Beginning Merchandise Inventory (Item A)	+	Purchases Of Merchandise (Item A)	=	Cost of Goods Available For Sale (Item A)	–	Ending Merchandise Inventory (Item A)	=	Cost of Goods Sold (Item A)
AA @ $166 = $166	+	(AB, AC) @ $375 + (AD, AE, AF, AG, AH) @ $800 = $1,175	=	$1,341	–	AC @ 187.50* AG @ 160** AH @ 160 $507.50	=	AA @ 166 AB @ 187.50 AD @ 160 AE @ 160 AF @ 160 $833.50

Computations

**$375 ÷ 2 = $187.50*

***$800 ÷ 5 = $160*

Management may have manipulated the inventory system to improve reported profits for January 2015. We would wonder why unit AC, which cost $187.50, was not sold in place of unit AD (cost of unit AD was only $160) on January 27 since both items were available for sale on that date. Management may have chosen to sell the item with the lower cost in order to minimize cost of goods sold for the month.

Notes

Chapter Three - Practicing with Current Assets

The Reason for This Chapter

Can you determine the appropriate value at which a corporation should carry its current assets? This chapter gives you the opportunity to do so. Completion of this chapter relies upon the accounting knowledge gained in *Fundamentals of Accounting: Volumes One, Two, and Three,* as well as *Accounting For Corporations: Volume One,* and also Chapters one and two of this book.

This Chapter consists of two case studies, each involving the same company, but they need help with their books. As an accountant, you will provide this aid.

In each case we will provide you with transactions, dates, and a brief summary of the company. And we will help you. To guide you through the accounting process we have provided blank forms for each case. All you must do is complete the forms provided!

What Do You Already Know?

In this section of the chapter we ask you to complete a pre-test. It will get you thinking about what you already know about accounting. It will also serve as a quick review of Chapters one and two.

If you have difficulties with the pre-test, you should go back and review the previous chapters. After completing the pre-test, check your answers against the ones provided. If they are correct, then complete the cases in this chapter.

Pre-Test

Question One

On October 8, 2014, Peekers Ltd. sold 5,000 units of inventory at a price of $3.25 each, on credit. On October 15, 2014, it replaced the sold inventory by ordering 8,000 units on account. The goods were shipped and the invoice received on October 15, 2014. The cost of these units has remained stable, at a price of $1.75 each, for the past year.

Prepare the necessary journal entries assuming Peekers Ltd. uses 1) the perpetual system, and 2) the periodic system. Use the space provided below:

Date	Debit	Credit

Computations:

Date	Debit	Credit

Computations:

Date	Debit	Credit

Computations:

Date	Debit	Credit

Computations:

Date	Debit	Credit

Question Two

On May 15, 2014, Excess Limited invested $50,000 of idle cash in a security. The brokerage fee for the transaction was $150. Management intends to sell the security within the next five months. On June 15, 2014 the security earned $2,500 worth of interest and the cash was received. Show the journal entries needed to record these transactions. Use the space provided below:

Excess Limited - General Journal

Date	Debit $	Credit $

Date	Debit	Credit

Answers to Pre-Test

Answer to Question One

As the cost of each unit has remained stable at $1.75, for the past year, no costing problem exits. We record Peekers Ltd.'s sale of goods, when the perpetual system is used, as follows:

Date October 8, 2014	**Debit**	**Credit**
Accounts Receivable	$16,250	
Sales Revenue		$16,250
To record the sale of 5,000 units on account at $3.25 each.		

Computations:
5,000 x $3.25 = $16,250.

Date October 8, 2014	**Debit**	**Credit**
Cost of Goods Sold	$8,750	
Inventory		$8,750
To record the use of 5,000 units to satisfy a sale, at a cost of $1.75 each.		

Computations:
5,000 x $1.75 = $8,750.

Under the periodic inventory system only the sale is recorded, before a physical count is made:

Date October 8, 2014	**Debit**	**Credit**
Accounts Receivable	$16,250	
Sales Revenue		$16,250
To record the sale of 5,000 units on account at $3.25 each.		

Computations:
5,000 x $3.25 = $16,250. Note, sales are the same regardless of the inventory system used.

We debit the Inventory account to record the purchase of goods for sale, when the perpetual system is used:

Date October 15, 2014	**Debit**	**Credit**
Inventory	$14,000	
Accounts Payable		$14,000
To record the purchase of 8,000 units on account at $1.75 each.		

Computations:
8,000 x $1.75 = $14,000.

And when a periodic system is used, we debit the Purchases account:

Date October 15, 2014	**Debit**	**Credit**
Purchases	$14,000	
Accounts Payable		$14,000
To record the purchase of 8,000 units on account at $1.75 each.		

Answer to Question Two

Excess Limited - General Journal

Date May 15, 2014	**Debit $**	**Credit $**
Temporary Investment	50,150	
Cash		50,150
To record the purchase of a temporary investment for $50,000 plus fee of $150.		

Date June 15, 2014	**Debit**	**Credit**
Cash	2,500	
Interest Revenue		2,500
To record interest earned on a temporary investment.		

How This Chapter Relates to Other Chapters in This Book

Chapters One and Two provided instruction on the proper value for reporting current assets on the balance sheet. In addition, it showed how to list current assets in order of their liquidity and provided a solid definition of a current asset. Two such assets were examined in detail; temporary investments and inventory.

The remaining chapters deal with the carrying value of capital or long-term assets, liabilities and preferred equity. This chapter and Chapter Six provide a review of these chapters. They are comprised of comprehensive cases that will enable you to demonstrate your accounting skills.

Topics Covered in Chapter Three

Case One
Yucan Ceramics Ltd. July 2014

Case Two
Yucan Ceramics Ltd. August 2014

Case One

Yucan Ceramics Ltd. July 2014

Yucan Ceramics Ltd. originally started as a potters guild in Mexico, over twenty years ago. The founder, Jose Yucan, moved the business to California in 2000. It flourished and was incorporated in 2005. All of Yucan's shares are privately held by the Yucan family. They also operate the business.

Yucan Ceramics Ltd. purchases and offers for resale handmade ceramic tiles. This material is ultimately used for indoor and patio floors. Yucan Ceramics sells to companies that apply finishing glazes to the tiles. The finished tiles are sold to building contractors and the public. Yucan's sales take place both at a store location and over the internet.

Jose Yucan started the business from next to nothing. It represents his life's work. He is the largest shareholder. During his many years in the business he had seen several competitors go bankrupt. Always concerned about getting into financial trouble, he avoided borrowing money wherever possible. Instead, the business retained all profits. Dividends have never been declared or paid. The equity is substantial.

Family members are rewarded with a salary for their efforts. Other workers receive wages. The business only uses short-term credit, such as purchasing merchandise inventory on account or income taxes payable. Excess cash is invested temporarily, usually for a period of 45 days or less.

Customers pay their accounts within 30 days, on average. Inventory takes 120 days to turn over, on average. The business uses the periodic system. Due to the unstable labor market, the purchase price of the handmade ceramic tiles is not stable. Yucan Ceramics always sells the oldest tiles first.

Yucan Ceramics Ltd. prepares financial statements at the end of each month. Their Post-Closing Trial Balance dated June 30, 2014 is as follows:

Yucan Ceramics Ltd.
Post-Closing Trial Balance
June 30, 2014

Account	Debit $	Credit $
Cash	28,400	
Temporary Investments	220,300	
Accounts Receivable	384,800	
Merchandise Inventory (872,000 units)	436,000	
Prepaid Insurance	10,500	
Equipment	420,000	
Accumulated Depreciation		68,000
Accounts Payable		166,200
Salaries Payable		80,000
Wages Payable		40,000
Income Taxes Payable		12,500
Share Capital		250,000
Retained Earnings		883,300
TOTAL	1,500,000	1,500,000

Transactions during July and additional information are as follows:

1. Purchased 100,000 tiles on account from suppliers in the amount of $70,000 at the beginning of July.
2. Sales, all on account, were 350,000 tiles at a price of $1.40 each, for the month.
3. Rent of $23,500 for the month of July is paid.
4. Total cash paid to employees in July is $120,000. This amount is for the salaries and wages that were owed at the end of June.
5. Various credit customers pay a total of $288,300 on their accounts during the month.
6. Yucan Ceramics pays $77,900 to its suppliers for accounts payable.
7. Miscellaneous expenses in the amount of $16,400 are paid in cash.
8. Purchased 200,000 tiles on account from suppliers in the amount of $180,000, at the end of July.

Information relating to Adjusting Entries and the Cost of Goods Schedule required at the end of the month is as follows:

9. The premium on a one-year insurance policy for the year September 1, 2013 to August 31, 2014 had been paid on September 1, 2013. At that time it cost $63,000.
10. Equipment is depreciated over a 25-year life. The estimated salvage value of the equipment is zero.
11. Employee salaries earned, but not yet paid at the end of July amount to $80,000. Wages earned but not paid during the month of July amount to $41,200.
12. A physical count at the end of July showed there were 800,000 tiles in inventory on 400 skids. Each skid or stack holds 2,000 tiles.
13. On July 31, 2014 the temporary investments had a market value of $210,000. A cash dividend of $10,300 had been declared and payment was expected within the next 45 days.
14. The company does not pay its income taxes each month. Instead, it reports the amount owed as Income Taxes Payable.

Each month the addition to Income Taxes Payable is calculated at the rate of 40% of income before taxes for that month. Hint: prepare this adjusting entry with the Closing Entries!

Today is July 31, 2014. As the bookkeeper for Yucan Ceramics Ltd. you are required to do the following:

a. Prepare the journal entries to record the transactions for July. The transactions have been accumulated so instead of recording the date, use the transaction number provided.

b. Set up T-accounts and enter the opening balances in the accounts from June 30, 2014. Post the entries from part (a) to the T-accounts, creating new ones as needed. Use the transaction numbers as a reference.

c. Prepare an unadjusted Trial Balance as of July 31, 2014.

d. Prepare the adjusting entries required at the end of July. Post them to their T-accounts.

e. Prepare an adjusted Trial Balance as of July 31, 2014.

f. Prepare the financial statements for the month of July.

g. Prepare and post the Closing Entries.

h. Prepare a Post-Closing Trial Balance.

i. Answer a question regarding inventory management. It is shown after part (h) in the pages that follow.

We have provided space to complete this work. Using these forms will help guide you through all the steps. If you have any space leftover then you have made an error!

Part a) JOURNAL ENTRIES:

Yucan Ceramics Ltd. – General Journal

Transaction # 1	$	$

Transaction # 2	$	$

Computations:

Transaction # 3	$	$

Transaction # 4	$	$

Computations:

Transaction # 5	$	$

Transaction # 6	$	$

Transaction # 7	$	$

Transaction # 8	$	$

Part b) POSTING TO THE LEDGER:

Yucan Ceramics Ltd. – General Ledger

Cash

Accounts Receivable

Temporary Investments

Merchandise Inventory

Prepaid Insurance

Equipment

Accum. Depreciation

Accounts Payable

Salaries Payable

Wages Payable

Income Taxes Payable

Share Capital

Retained Earnings

Sales Revenue

Purchases

Rent Expense

Miscellaneous Expense

Part c) PREPARING THE UNADJUSTED TRIAL BALANCE:

Yucan Ceramics Ltd.
Unadjusted Trial Balance
As at July 31, 2014

Account	Debit $	Credit $
TOTAL		

Part d) ADJUSTING ENTRIES

Yucan Ceramics Ltd. – General Journal

	$	$

Computations:

	$	$

Computations:

	$	$

	$	$

	$	$

Computation:

	$	$

Note: We have provided the permanent account titles and balances needed for the adjusting entries.

Yucan Ceramics Ltd. – General Ledger

Prepaid Insurance

Bal. 10,500	

Accumulated Depreciation

	68,000 Bal.

Salaries Payable

(#4) 80,000	*80,000 Bal.*
	0 Bal.

Wages Payable

(#4) 40,000	*40,000 Bal.*
	0 Bal.

Temporary Investments

Bal. 220,300	

Dividend Revenue Receivable

Part e) ADJUSTED TRIAL BALANCE:

Yucan Ceramics Ltd.
Adjusted Trial Balance
July 31, 2014

Account	Debit $	Credit $
TOTAL		

Part f) FINANCIAL STATEMENTS:

First, Complete the Cost of Goods Sold Schedule:

Beginning Merchandise Inventory (Item A)	+	Purchases Of Merchandise (Item A)	=	Cost of Goods Available For Sale (Item A)	–	Ending Merchandise Inventory (Item A)	=	Cost of Goods Sold (Item A)

Yucan Ceramics Ltd.
Income Statement
For the month ended July 31, 2014

Sales Revenue		
Less: Cost of Goods Sold		
Gross Profit		
Operating Expenses:		
Rent Expense		
Salaries Expense		
Wages Expense		
Insurance Expense		
Depreciation Expense		
Miscellaneous Expense		
Total Operating Expenses		
Operating Income		
Dividend Revenue		
Unrealized Holding Loss on Temporary Investments		
Income before Income Taxes		
Income Tax Expense (40%)		
Net Income		

Yucan Ceramics Ltd.
Balance Sheet
As at July 31, 2014

ASSETS	$
TOTAL ASSETS	
LIABILITIES	
OWNERS' EQUITY	
TOTAL LIABILITIES AND OWNERS' EQUITY	

Part g) CLOSING ENTRIES:

First, prepare the Adjusting Entry for Income Taxes:

Yucan Ceramics Ltd. – General Journal – Adjusting Entries

July 31, 2014- Transaction #14	$	$
Income Tax Expense		
Income Taxes Payable		
To record the income tax expense for the month of July.		

Computation: *obtained from the Income Statement.*

Next, prepare all Closing Entries:

Yucan Ceramics Ltd. – General Journal – Closing Entries

July 31, 2014	$	$

July 31, 2014	$	$

July 31, 2014	$	$
Income Summary		
Merchandise Inventory		
To transfer the beginning inventory balance to Income Summary.		

July 31, 2014	$	$
Income Summary		
Purchases		
To transfer the Purchases balance to Income Summary.		

July 31, 2014	$	$
Merchandise Inventory		
Income Summary		
To transfer the ending inventory balance to Income Summary and account for Cost of Goods Sold through Income Summary.		

	$	$

	$	$

	$	$

	$	$

	$	$

	$	$

	$	$

	$	$

July 31, 2014	$	$
Income Summary		
Retained Earnings		
To close the Income Summary to Retained Earnings.		

Posting to the Ledger: The first balances shown are from the Adjusted Trial Balance.

Cash	
Bal. 78,900	

Accounts Receivable	
Bal. 586,500	

Dividend Revenue Receivable	
Bal. 10,300	

Temporary Investments	
Bal. 210,000	

Merchandise Inventory	
Bal. 436,000	

Prepaid Insurance	
Bal. 5,250	

Equipment	
Bal. 420,000	

Accumulated Depreciation	
	69,400 Bal.

Accounts Payable	
	338,300 Bal.

Salaries Payable	
	80,000 Bal.

Wages Payable	
	41,200 Bal.

Income Taxes Payable	
	12,500 Bal.

Share Capital

	250,000 Bal.

Retained Earnings

	883,300 Bal.

Sales Revenue

	490,000 Bal.

Purchases

Bal. 250,000	

Rent Expense

Bal. 23,500	

Salaries Expense

Bal. 80,000	

Wages Expense

Bal. 41,200	

Insurance Expense

Bal. 5,250	

Depreciation Expense

Bal. 1,400	

Miscellaneous Expense

Bal. 16,400	

Dividend Revenue

	10,300 Bal.

Unrealized Holding Loss on Temporary Investments

Bal. 10,300	

Income Tax Expense

Income Summary

Part h) POST-CLOSING TRIAL BALANCE:

Yucan Ceramics Ltd.
Post-Closing Trial Balance
As at July 31, 2014

Account	Debit $	Credit $
TOTAL		

Part i) INVENTORY QUESTION:

With regards to the number of units in ending inventory and those sold during the month of July, is there an inventory management problem at Yucan Ceramics Ltd.? Explain.

Solution to Case One:

Part a) JOURNAL ENTRIES:

Yucan Ceramics Ltd. – General Journal

Transaction # 1	*$*	*$*
Purchases	*70,000*	
Accounts Payable		*70,000*
To record the purchase of 100,000 tiles on account.		

Transaction # 2	*$*	*$*
Accounts Receivable	*490,000*	
Sales Revenue		*490,000*
To record the sales, all on account, for July.		

Computations:
350,000 x $1.40 = $490,000

Transaction # 3	*$*	*$*
Rent Expense	*23,500*	
Cash		*23,500*
To record the payment of rent for July.		

Transaction # 4	*$*	*$*
Salaries Payable	*80,000*	
Wages Payable	*40,000*	
Cash		*120,000*
To record the salaries and wages paid during July.		

Computations:
The salaries and wages payable at the end of June amount to $80,000 + $40,000 = $120,000

Transaction # 5	*$*	*$*
Cash	*288,300*	
Accounts Receivable		*288,300*
To record cash received from customers for payment on their accounts.		

Transaction # 6	$	$
Accounts payable	*77,900*	
Cash		*77,900*
To record payment on account to suppliers.		

Transaction # 7	$	$
Miscellaneous Expense	*16,400*	
Cash		*16,400*
To record payment of miscellaneous expenses		

Transaction # 8	$	$
Purchases	*180,000*	
Accounts Payable		*180,000*
To record the purchase of 200,000 tiles on account.		

Part b) POSTING TO THE LEDGER:

Yucan Ceramics Ltd. – General Ledger

Cash	
Bal. 28,400	23,500 (#3)
(#5) 288,300	120,000 (#4)
	77,900 (#6)
	16,400 (#7)
Bal. 78,900	

Accounts Receivable	
Bal. 384,800	288,300 (#5)
(#2) 490,000	
Bal. 586,500	

Temporary Investments	
Bal. 220,300	

Merchandise Inventory	
Bal. 436,000	

Prepaid Insurance	
Bal. 10,500	

Equipment	
Bal. 420,000	

Accum. Depreciation	
	68,000 Bal.

Accounts Payable	
(#6) 77,900	166,200 Bal.
	70,000 (#1)
	180,000 (#8)
	338,300 Bal.

Salaries Payable	
(#4) 80,000	80,000 Bal.
	0 Bal.

Wages Payable

(#4) 40,000	40,000 Bal.
	Bal. 0

Income Taxes Payable

	12,500 Bal.

Share Capital

	250,000 Bal.

Retained Earnings

	883,300 Bal.

Sales Revenue

	490,000 (#2)

Purchases

(#1) 70,000	
(#8) 180,000	
250,000	

Rent Expense

(#3) 23,500	

Miscellaneous Expense

(#7) 16,400	

Part c) PREPARING THE UNADJUSTED TRIAL BALANCE:

Yucan Ceramics Ltd.
Unadjusted Trial Balance
As at July 31, 2014

Account	Debit $	Credit $
Cash	78,900	
Temporary Investments	220,300	
Accounts Receivable	586,500	
Merchandise Inventory	436,000	
Prepaid Insurance	10,500	
Equipment	420,000	
Accumulated Depreciation		68,000
Accounts Payable		338,300
Income Taxes Payable		12,500
Share Capital		250,000
Retained Earnings		883,300
Sales Revenue		490,000
Purchases	250,000	
Rent Expense	23,500	
Miscellaneous Expense	16,400	
TOTAL	2,042,100	2,042,100

Part d) ADJUSTING ENTRIES:

Yucan Ceramics Ltd. – General Journal

July 31, 2014 - Transaction #9	$	$
Insurance Expense	5,250	
Prepaid Insurance		5,250
To record the insurance expense for the month of July		

Computations:

$63,000 ÷ 12 months = $5,250 per month, OR on June 30 there are two months remaining on the policy for a total of $10,500: $10,500 ÷ 2 = $5,250 per month.

July 31, 2014- - Transaction #10	$	$
Depreciation Expense	1,400	
Accumulated Depreciation		1,400
To record the depreciation expense for the month of July.		

Computations:

($420,000 - $0) ÷ 25 years = $16,800 per year.
$16, 800 ÷ 12 months = $1,400 per month.

July 31, 2014 - Transaction #11	$	$
Salaries Expense	80,000	
Salaries Payable		80,000
To record salaries earned, but not yet paid at the end of July.		

July 31, 2014 - Transaction #11	$	$
Wages Expense	41,200	
Wages Payable		41,200
To record wages earned, but not yet paid at the end of July.		

Transaction #12 : No adjusting entry is made as the merchandise inventory and purchases accounts will be closed to income summary. Under the periodic method we do not need to have a Cost of Goods Sold account in the ledger. We encourage you to refer back to Chapter Two of this book to review this system.

July 31, 2014 - Transaction #13	$	$
Unrealized Holding Loss on Temporary Investments	*10,300*	
Temporary Investments		*10,300*
To reduce temporary investments to Lower of Cost and Market.		

Computation:
$220,300 - $210,000 = $10,300.

July 31, 2014 - Transaction #13	$	$
Dividend Revenue Receivable	*$10,300*	
Dividend Revenue		*10,300*
To record a cash dividend receivable relating to temporary investments.		

Note to the student: *It is merely a coincidence that the unrealized holding loss and the dividend revenue are the same figure.*

Yucan Ceramics Ltd. – General Ledger

Prepaid Insurance

Bal. 10,500	5,250 (#9)
Bal. 5,250	

Insurance Expense

(#9) 5,250	

Accumulated Depreciation

	68,000 Bal.
	1,400 (#10)
	69,400 Bal.

Depreciation Expense

(#10) 1,400	

Salaries Payable

	0 Bal.
	80,000 (#11)

Salaries Expense

(#11) 80,000	

Wages Payable

	0 Bal.
	41,200 (#11)

Wages Expense

(#11) 41,200	

Temporary Investments

Bal. 220,300	10,300 (#13)
Bal. 210,000	

Unrealized Holding Loss on Temporary Investments

(#13) 10,300	

Dividend Revenue Receivable

Bal. 0	
(#13) 10,300	

Dividend Revenue

	10,300 (#13)

Part e) ADJUSTED TRIAL BALANCE:

Yucan Ceramics Ltd.
Adjusted Trial Balance
July 31, 2014

Account	Debit $	Credit $
Cash	78,900	
Temporary Investments	210,000	
Accounts Receivable	586,500	
Dividend Revenue Receivable	10,300	
Merchandise Inventory	436,000	
Prepaid Insurance	5,250	
Equipment	420,000	
Accumulated Depreciation		69,400
Accounts Payable		338,300
Salaries Payable		80,000
Wages Payable		41,200
Income Taxes Payable		12,500
Share Capital		250,000
Retained Earnings		883,300
Sales Revenue		490,000
Dividend Revenue		10,300
Purchases	250,000	
Rent Expense	23,500	
Salaries Expense	80,000	
Wages Expense	41,200	
Insurance Expense	5,250	
Depreciation Expense	1,400	
Unrealized Holding Loss on Temporary Investments	10,300	
Miscellaneous Expense	16,400	
TOTAL	2,175,000	2,175,000

Part f) FINANCIAL STATEMENTS:

First, complete the Cost of Goods Sold Schedule:

Beginning Merchandise Inventory (Item A)		Purchases Of Merchandise (Item A)		Cost of Goods Available For Sale (Item A)		Ending Merchandise Inventory (Item A)		Cost of Goods Sold (Item A)
$436,000; 872,000 units @$0.50*	+	$250.000; 100,000 units @ $0.70**+ 200,000@ $0.90***	=	$686,000; 1,172,000 units available	–	$500,000; 800,000 newest units remaining: (200,000 units @ $0.90) + (100,000 @ $0.70) + (500,000 @ $0.50) = $500,000	=	186,000

From the June post-closing trial balance and the July general journal we obtain the information needed to calculate the price per unit so we may use it to value the ending inventory:
**$436,000 ÷ 872,000 = $0.50 per unit.*
***$70,000 ÷ 100,000 = $0.70 per unit.*
****$180,000 ÷ 200,000 = $0.90 per unit.*

Under FIFO, we must determine the ending inventory value using the assumption that the oldest units were sold first, and therefore the newest units remain in inventory. The physical count showed 800,000 tiles remained at the end of the month. They must be the newest units. Thus, before we can post the closing entries we must value the ending inventory under FIFO. We have done so in the Cost of Goods Sold Schedule, above.

Yucan Ceramics Ltd.
Income Statement
For the month ended July 31, 2014

Sales Revenue		$490,000
Less: Cost of Goods Sold*		186,000
Gross Profit		304,000
Operating Expenses:		
Rent Expense	$23,500	
Salaries Expense	80,000	
Wages Expense	41,200	
Insurance Expense	5,250	
Depreciation Expense	1,400	
Miscellaneous Expense	16,400	
Total Operating Expenses		(167,750)
Operating Income		136,250
Dividend Revenue		10,300
Unrealized Holding Loss on Temporary Investments		(10,300)**
Income before Income Taxes		136,250
Income Tax Expense (40%)		54,500
Net Income		**$81,750**

*From Cost of Goods Sold Schedule.
**We will ignore the true tax treatment of this unrealized holding loss. We remind you it is a coincidence that the dividend revenue and unrealized holding loss net to zero.

Yucan Ceramics Ltd.
Balance Sheet
As at July 31, 2014

ASSETS		$
Cash		78,900
Temporary Investments		210,000
Account Receivable		586,500
Dividend Revenue Receivable		10,300
Merchandise Inventory*		500,000
Prepaid Insurance		5,250
Equipment	$420,000	
Less: Accumulated Depreciation	(69,400)	350,600
TOTAL ASSETS		**1,741,550**
LIABILITIES		
Accounts Payable		338,300
Salaries Payable		80,000
Wages Payable		41,200
Income Taxes Payable**		67,000
Total Liabilities		526,500
OWNERS' EQUITY		
Share Capital		250,000
Retained Earnings***		965,050
Total Owners' Equity		1,215,050
TOTAL LIABILITIES AND OWNERS' EQUITY		**1,741,550**

*The inventory remaining on July 31, 2014 must be the Ending Inventory as per the Cost of Goods Sold Schedule.

**Income Taxes Payable includes Income Tax Expense for July: $12,500 + $54,500 = $67,000.

***$883,300 + $81,750 = $965,050.

NOTE: *the order of assets on the balance sheet is according to their liquidity.*

Part g) CLOSING ENTRIES:

First, the Adjusting Entry for Income Taxes:

Yucan Ceramics Ltd. – General Journal

July 31, 2014- Transaction #14	$	$
Income Tax Expense	54,500	
Income Taxes Payable		54,500
To record the income tax expense for the month of July.		

Computation: *obtained from the Income Statement.*

Next, all Closing Entries:

Yucan Ceramics Ltd. – General Journal – Closing Entries

July 31, 2014	$	$
Sales Revenue	490,000	
Income Summary		490,000
To close Sales Revenue to Income Summary.		

July 31, 2014	$	$
Dividend Revenue	10,300	
Income Summary		10,300
To close Dividend Revenue to Income Summary.		

July 31, 2014	$	$
Income Summary	436,000	
Merchandise Inventory		436,000
To transfer the beginning inventory balance to Income Summary.		

July 31, 2014	$	$
Income Summary	250,000	
Purchases		250,000
To transfer the Purchases balance to Income Summary.		

July 31, 2014	$	$
Merchandise Inventory	500,000	
Income Summary		500,000
To transfer the ending inventory balance to Income Summary and account for Cost of Goods Sold through Income Summary.		

July 31, 2014	$	$
Income Summary	23,500	
Rent Expense		23,500
To close the Rent Expense to Income Summary.		

July 31, 2014	$	$
Income Summary	80,000	
Salaries Expense		80,000
To close the Salaries Expense to Income Summary.		

July 31, 2014	$	$
Income Summary	41,200	
Wages Expense		41,200
To close the Wages Expense to Income Summary.		

July 31, 2014	$	$
Income Summary	5,250	
Insurance Expense		5,250
To close the Insurance Expense to Income Summary.		

July 31, 2014	$	$
Income Summary	1,400	
Depreciation Expense		1,400
To close the Depreciation Expense to Income Summary.		

July 31, 2014	$	$
Income Summary	16,400	
Miscellaneous Expense		16,400
To close the Miscellaneous Expense to Income Summary.		

July 31, 2014	$	$
Income Summary	*10,300*	
Unrealized Holding Loss on Temporary Investments		*10,300*
To close the Unrealized Holding Loss on Temporary Investments to Income Summary.		

July 31, 2014	$	$
Income Summary	*54,500*	
Income Tax Expense		*54,500*
To close the Income Tax Expense to Income Summary.		

July 31, 2014	$	$
Income Summary	*81,750*	
Retained Earnings		*81,750*
To close the Income Summary to Retained Earnings.		

Posting to the Ledger: The first balances shown are from the Adjusted Trial Balance.

Cash	
Bal. 78,900	

Accounts Receivable	
Bal. 586,500	

Dividend Revenue Receivable	
Bal. 10,300	

Temporary Investments	
Bal. 210,000	

Merchandise Inventory	
Bal. 436,000	*436,000 close*
End 500,000	
Bal. 500,000	

Prepaid Insurance	
Bal. 5,250	

Equipment	
Bal. 420,000	

Accumulated Depreciation	
	69,400 Bal.

Accounts Payable	
	338,300 Bal.

Salaries Payable	
	80,000 Bal.

Wages Payable	
	41,200 Bal.

Income Taxes Payable	
	12,500 Bal.
	54,500 (adjusting)
	67,000 Bal.

Share Capital

	250,000 Bal.

Retained Earnings

	883,300 Bal.
	81,750 close
	965,050 Bal.

Sales Revenue

close 490,000	490,000 Bal.

Purchases

Bal. 250,000	250,000 close

Rent Expense

Bal. 23,500	23,500 close

Salaries Expense

Bal. 80,000	80,000 close

Wages Expense

Bal. 41,200	41,200 close

Insurance Expense

Bal. 5,250	5,250 close

Depreciation Expense

Bal. 1,400	1,400 close

Miscellaneous Expense

Bal. 16,400	16,400 close

Dividend Revenue

close 10,300	10,300 Bal.

Unrealized Holding Loss on Temporary Investments

Bal. 10,300	10,300 close

Income Tax Expense

adjust. 54,500	54,500 close

Income Summary

		490,000	Sales
Beginning Inventory	436,000	500,000	Ending Inventory
Purchases	250,000		

Note: the difference here is Gross Profit of $304,000!

		10,300	Dividend Revenue
Rent	23,500		
Salaries	80,000		
Wages	41,200		
Insurance	5,250		
Depreciation	1,400		
Miscellaneous	16,400		
Unrealized loss	10,300		
Income Tax	54,500		
		81,750 Bal.	
	Close 81,750	Note: this is Net Income, we credit it to Retained Earnings.	

Part h) POST-CLOSING TRIAL BALANCE:

Yucan Ceramics Ltd.
Post-Closing Trial Balance
As at July 31, 2014

Account	Debit $	Credit $
Cash	78,900	
Temporary Investments	210,000	
Accounts Receivable	586,500	
Dividend Revenue Receivable	10,300	
Merchandise Inventory	500,000	
Prepaid Insurance	5,250	
Equipment	420,000	
Accumulated Depreciation		69,400
Accounts Payable		338,300
Salaries Payable		80,000
Wages Payable		41,200
Income Taxes Payable		67,000
Share Capital		250,000
Retained Earnings		965,050
TOTAL	1,810,950	1,810,950

Part i) INVENTORY QUESTION:

Yucan Ceramics Ltd. should be concerned about inventory management. Refer back to the Cost of Goods Sold Schedule; we showed units as well as the dollars. According to the schedule there were 1,172,000 units available for sale. The case specifically tells us 350,000 units were sold. The difference of 822,000 tiles should be in ending inventory. When the physical units are counted at the end of July, there are only 800,000 tiles actually on hand. Therefore, 22,000 tiles are missing!

Because the periodic system assigns spoiled or stolen inventory as cost of good sold, the missing tiles could go unnoticed. In this case the ending inventory of 800,000 tiles means the company will assume that 372,000 tiles were sold, when in fact only 350,000 were actually sold. Should the company manage only the dollars and not the units, the problem may continue to go unobserved.

Case Two

Yucan Ceramics Ltd. August 2014

Due to the large inventory loss in July (remember 22,000 tiles were unaccounted for) the accountant for Yucan Ceramics Ltd. went into the warehouse on August 1, 2014. She questioned the manager about the physical flow of tiles. He reported that since all the tiles physically look the same, newly shipped orders are simply added to the existing inventory. No attempt is made to move the oldest tiles out first, nor the newest tiles out first. Tiles cannot be specifically identified. The movement of tiles is random.

As a result of this discussion, the accountant at Yucan Ceramics Ltd. has requested that two changes be made: (1) use a different inventory costing method to evaluate ending inventory for the month of August and (2) adopt the perpetual system of inventory management.

Jose Yucan, the President and largest shareholder instantly approved the first request. It will be implemented immediately. For the month of August the inventory costing method will definitely not be FIFO.

The second change will entail a large monetary expenditure. Jose is still contemplating this request. Until it is approved, and a new computer system installed, the periodic system must still be used.

Yucan Ceramics Ltd. prepares financial statements at the end of each month. Their Post-Closing Trial Balance dated July 31, 2014 (from Case One) is as follows:

Yucan Ceramics Ltd.
Post-Closing Trial Balance
As at July 31, 2014

Account	Debit $	Credit $
Cash	78,900	
Temporary Investments	210,000	
Accounts Receivable	586,500	
Dividend Revenue Receivable	10,300	
Merchandise Inventory (800,000 tiles)	500,000	
Prepaid Insurance	5,250	
Equipment	420,000	
Accumulated Depreciation		69,400
Accounts Payable		338,300
Salaries Payable		80,000
Wages Payable		41,200
Income Taxes Payable		67,000
Share Capital		250,000
Retained Earnings		965,050
TOTAL	1,810,950	1,810,950

Transactions during August and additional information are as follows:

1. Purchased 100,000 tiles on account from suppliers in the amount of $90,000 at the beginning of August.
2. Sales, all on account, were 480,000 tiles at a price of $1.40 each, for the month.
3. Rent of $23,500 for the month of August is paid.
4. Total cash paid to employees in August is $121,200. This amount is for the salaries and wages that were owed at the end of July.
5. Various credit customers pay a total of $300,000 on their accounts during the month.

6. Yucan Ceramics pays $100,000 to its suppliers for accounts payable.
7. Miscellaneous expenses in the amount of $15,800 are paid in cash.
8. Purchased 50,000 tiles on account from suppliers in the amount of $50,000, at the end of August.
9. Purchased, and paid for, an insurance policy for $63,000 from September 1, 2014 through August 31, 2015.
10. The Dividend Revenue of $10,300 from July was received in cash.
11. On August 31, 2014 the temporary investments were sold for $200,000.

Information relating to Adjusting Entries and the Cost of Goods Schedule required at the end of the month is as follows:

12. The premium on a one-year insurance policy for the year September 1, 2013 to August 31, 2014 had been paid on September 1, 2013. At that time it cost $63,000.
13. Equipment is depreciated over a 25-year life. The estimated salvage value of the equipment is zero.
14. Employee salaries earned, but not yet paid at the end of August amount to $80,000. Wages earned but not paid during the month of August amount to $45,200.
15. A physical count at the end of August showed there were 460,000 tiles in inventory on 230 skids. Each skid or stack holds 2,000 tiles.
16. The company does not pay its income taxes each month. Instead, it reports the amount owed as Income Taxes Payable. Each month the addition to Income Taxes Payable is calculated at the rate of 40% of income before taxes for that month. Hint: prepare this adjusting entry with the Closing Entries!

Today is August 31, 2014. As the bookkeeper for Yucan Ceramics Ltd. you are required to do the following:

a. Prepare the journal entries to record the transactions for August. The transactions have been accumulated so instead of recording the date, use the transaction number provided.

b. Set up T-accounts and enter the opening balances in the accounts from July 31, 2014. Post the entries from part (a) to the T-accounts, creating new ones as needed. Use the transaction numbers as a reference.

c. Prepare an unadjusted Trial Balance as of August 31, 2014.

d. Prepare the adjusting entries required at the end of August. Post them to their T-accounts.

e. Prepare an adjusted Trial Balance as of August 31, 2014.

f. Prepare the financial statements for the month of August.

g. Prepare and post the Closing Entries.

h. Prepare a Post-Closing Trial Balance.

i. Answer a question regarding inventory management. It is shown after part (h) in the pages that follow.

We have provided space to complete this work. Using these forms will help guide you through all the steps. If you have any space leftover then you have made an error!

Part a) JOURNAL ENTRIES:

Yucan Ceramics Ltd. – General Journal

	$	$

	$	$

Computation:

	$	$

	$	$

Computation:

	$	$

	$	$

	$	$

	$	$

	$	$

	$	$

	$	$

Computation:

Part b) POSTING TO THE LEDGER:

Yucan Ceramics Ltd. – General Ledger

Cash

Accounts Receivable

Dividend Revenue Receivable

Temporary Investments

Merchandise Inventory

Prepaid Insurance

Equipment

Accumulated Depreciation

Accounts Payable

Salaries Payable

Wages Payable

Income Taxes Payable

Share Capital

Retained Earnings

Part c) PREPARING THE UNADJUSTED TRIAL BALANCE:

Yucan Ceramics Ltd.
Unadjusted Trial Balance
As at August 31, 2014

Account	Debit $	Credit $
TOTAL		

Part d) ADJUSTING ENTRIES and other transactions:

Yucan Ceramics Ltd. – General Journal

	$	$

Computations:

	$	$

Computations:

	$	$

	$	$

Yucan Ceramics Ltd. – General Ledger

Note: we have provided the permanent account titles and balances, to date.

Prepaid Insurance

Bal. 68,250	

Accumulated Depreciation

	69,400 bal.

Salaries Payable

Wages Payable

Part e) ADJUSTED TRIAL BALANCE:

Yucan Ceramics Ltd.
Adjusted Trial Balance
August 31, 2014

Account	Debit $	Credit $
TOTAL		

Part f) FINANCIAL STATEMENTS:

First, recognize the appropriate method is weighted average. Compute the weighted average cost per unit:

Cost of Goods Available for Sale	Number of Units Available for Sale	Explanation
		Beginning inventory balance
		Purchase transaction #1
		Purchase transaction #8
		TOTALS

Computing the weighted average cost per unit:

____

Then, calculate Ending Inventory based on the weighted average method:

Beginning Merchandise Inventory (Item A)		Purchases Of Merchandise (Item A)		Cost of Goods Available For Sale (Item A)		Ending Merchandise Inventory (Item A)		Cost of Goods Sold (Item A)
	+		=		–		=	

Yucan Ceramics Ltd.
Income Statement
For the month ended August 31, 2014

Gross Profit		
Operating Expenses:		
Total Operating Expenses		
Total Expenses		
Income before Income Taxes		
Income Tax Expense (40%)		
Net Income		

Yucan Ceramics Ltd.
Balance Sheet
As at August 31, 2014

ASSETS	$
TOTAL ASSETS	
LIABILITIES	
OWNERS' EQUITY	
TOTAL LIABILITIES AND OWNERS' EQUITY	

Part g) CLOSING ENTRIES:

First, prepare the Adjusting Entry for Income Taxes:

Yucan Ceramics Ltd. – General Journal

	$	$

Computation:

Next, prepare all Closing Entries

Yucan Ceramics Ltd. – General Journal – Closing Entries

	$	$

	$	$

	$	$

	$	$

	$	$

	$	$

	$	$

	$	$

	$	$

	$	$

	$	$

	$	$

	$	$

Posting to the Ledger: The first balances shown are from the Adjusted Trial Balance.

Cash	
Bal. 265,700	

Accounts Receivable	
Bal. 958,500	

Merchandise Inventory	
Bal. 500,000	

Prepaid Insurance	
Bal. 63,000	

Equipment	
Bal. 420,000	

Accumulated Depreciation	
	70,800 Bal.

Accounts Payable	
	378,300 Bal.

Salaries Payable	
	80,000 Bal.

Wages Payable	
	45,200 Bal.

Income Taxes Payable	
	67,000 Bal.

Share Capital	
	250,000 Bal.

Retained Earnings	
	965,050 Bal.

Sales Revenue	
	672,000 Bal.

Purchases	
Bal. 140,000	

Rent Expense	
Bal. 23,500	

Salaries Expense	
Bal. 80,000	

Wages Expense	
Bal. 45,200	

Insurance Expense	
Bal. 5,250	

Depreciation Expense	
Bal. 1,400	

Miscellaneous Expense	
Bal. 15,800	

Realized Loss on Sale of Temporary Investments	
Bal. 10,000	

Income Tax Expense

Income Summary

Part h) POST-CLOSING TRIAL BALANCE:

Yucan Ceramics Ltd.
Post-Closing Trial Balance
As at August 31, 2014

Account	Debit $	Credit $
TOTAL		

Part i) INVENTORY QUESTION:

With regards to the new inventory costing method, did the weighted average approach provide better control than FIFO, used in Case One? Explain.

Solution to Case Two:

Part a) JOURNAL ENTRIES:

Yucan Ceramics Ltd. – General Journal

Transaction # 1	$	$
Purchases	90,000	
Accounts Payable		90,000
To record the purchase of 100,000 tiles on account.		

Transaction #2	$	$
Accounts Receivable	672,000	
Sales Revenue		672,000
To record the sales, all on account, for August.		

Computation:

480,000 x $1.40 = $672,000.

Transaction #3	$	$
Rent Expense	23,500	
Cash		23,500
To record the payment of rent for August.		

Transaction #4	$	$
Salaries Payable	80,000	
Wages Payable	41,200	
Cash		121,200
To record the salaries and wages paid during August.		

Computation:

The salaries and wages payable at the end of July amount to $80,000 + $41,200 = $121,200.

Transaction #5	$	$
Cash	300,000	
Accounts Receivable		300,000
To record cash received from customers for payment on their accounts.		

Transaction #6	$	$
Accounts Payable	100,000	
Cash		100,000
To record payment on account to suppliers.		

Transaction # 7	$	$
Miscellaneous Expense	15,800	
Cash		15,800
To record the cash payment of miscellaneous expenses.		

Transaction # 8	$	$
Purchases	50,000	
Accounts Payable		50,000
To record the purchase of 50,000 tiles on account.		

Transaction # 9	$	$
Prepaid Insurance	63,000	
Cash		63,000
To record the purchase of an insurance policy from September 1, 2014 through August 31, 2015.		

Transaction # 10	$	$
Cash	10,300	
Dividend Revenue Receivable		10,300
To record the receipt of the dividend revenue from July.		

August 31, 2014- - Transaction #11	$	$
Cash	200,000	
Realized Loss on Sale of Temporary Investments	10,000	
Temporary Investments		210,000
To record the loss realized on the sale of temporary investments.		

Computation:

$210,000 - $200,000 = $10,000 loss.

Part b) POSTING TO THE LEDGER:

Yucan Ceramics Ltd. – General Ledger

Cash

Bal. 78,900	23,500 (#3)
(#5) 300,000	121,200 (#4)
(#10) 10,300	100,000 (#6)
	15,800 (#7)
(#11) 200,000	63,000 (#9)
Bal. 265,700	

Accounts Receivable

Bal. 586,500	300,000 (#5)
(#2) 672,000	
Bal. 958,500	

Dividend Revenue Receivable

Bal. 10,300	10,300 (#10)
Bal. 0	

Temporary Investments

Bal. 210,000	210,000 (#11)
Bal. 0	

Merchandise Inventory

Bal. 500,000	

Prepaid Insurance

Bal. 5,250	
(#9) 63,000	
Bal. 68,250	

Equipment

Bal. 420,000	

Accumulated Depreciation

	69,400 Bal.

Accounts Payable

(#6) 100,000	338,300 Bal.
	90,000 (#1)
	50,000 (#8)
	378,300 Bal.

Salaries Payable

(#4) 80,000	80,000 Bal.
	0 Bal.

Wages Payable

(#4) 41,200	41,200 Bal.
	Bal. 0

Income Taxes Payable

	67,000 Bal.

Share Capital

	250,000 Bal.

Retained Earnings

	965,050 Bal.

Sales Revenue

	672,000 (#2)

Purchases

(#1) 90,000	
(#8) 50,000	

Rent Expense

(#3) 23,500	

Miscellaneous Expense

(#7) 15,800	

Realized Loss on Sale of Temporary Investments

(#11) 10,000	

Part c) PREPARING THE UNADJUSTED TRIAL BALANCE:

Yucan Ceramics Ltd.
Unadjusted Trial Balance
As at August 31, 2014

Account	Debit $	Credit $
Cash	265,700	
Accounts Receivable	958,500	
Merchandise Inventory	500,000	
Prepaid Insurance	68,250	
Equipment	420,000	
Accumulated Depreciation		69,400
Accounts Payable		378,300
Income Taxes Payable		67,000
Share Capital		250,000
Retained Earnings		965,050
Sales Revenue		672,000
Purchases	140,000	
Rent Expense	23,500	
Miscellaneous Expense	15,800	
Realized Loss on Sale of Temporary Investments	10,000	
TOTAL	2,401,750	2,401,750

Part d) ADJUSTING ENTRIES and Other transactions

Yucan Ceramics Ltd. – General Journal

August 31, 2014 - Transaction #12	$	$
Insurance Expense	5,250	
Prepaid Insurance		5,250
To record the insurance expense for the month of August.		

Computations:

$63,000 ÷ 12 months = $5,250 per month, OR on July 31 there is one month remaining on the policy for a total of $5,250 per month. The new policy is not effective until September.

August 31, 2014 - Transaction #13	*$*	*$*
Depreciation Expense	*1,400*	
Accumulated Depreciation		*1,400*
To record the depreciation expense for the month of August.		

Computations:

(\$420,000 - \$0) ÷ 25 years = \$16,800 per year.

\$16, 800 ÷ 12 months = \$1,400 per month.

August 31, 2014 - Transaction #14	*$*	*$*
Salaries Expense	*80,000*	
Salaries Payable		*80,000*
To record salaries earned, but not yet paid at the end of August.		

August 31, 2014 - Transaction #14	*$*	*$*
Wages Expense	*45,200*	
Wages Payable		*45,200*
To record wages earned, but not yet paid at the end of August.		

Transaction #15 : No adjusting entry is made as the merchandise inventory and purchase accounts will be closed to income summary. Under the periodic method we do not need to have a Cost of Goods Sold account in the ledger. We encourage you to refer back to Chapter Two of this book to review this system.

Yucan Ceramics Ltd. – General Ledger

Prepaid Insurance

Bal. 68,250	*5,250 (#12)*
Bal. 63,000	

Insurance Expense

(#12) 5,250	

Accumulated Depreciation

	69,400 bal.
	1,400 (#13)
	70,800 Bal.

Depreciation Expense

(#13) 1,400	

Salaries Payable

	80,000 (#14)

Salaries Expense

(#14) 80,000	

Wages Payable

	45,200 (#14)

Wages Expense

(#14) 45,200	

Part e) ADJUSTED TRIAL BALANCE:

Yucan Ceramics Ltd.
Adjusted Trial Balance
August 31, 2014

Account	Debit $	Credit $
Cash	265,700	
Accounts Receivable	958,500	
Merchandise Inventory	500,000	
Prepaid Insurance	63,000	
Equipment	420,000	
Accumulated Depreciation		70,800
Accounts Payable		378,300
Salaries Payable		80,000
Wages Payable		45,200
Income Taxes Payable		67,000
Share Capital		250,000
Retained Earnings		965,050
Sales Revenue		672,000
Purchases	140,000	
Rent Expense	23,500	
Salaries Expense	80,000	
Wages Expense	45,200	
Insurance Expense	5,250	
Depreciation Expense	1,400	
Miscellaneous Expense	15,800	
Realized Loss on Sale of Temporary Investments	10,000	
TOTAL	2,528,350	2,528,350

Part f) FINANCIAL STATEMENTS:

You must recognize that the accountant has selected the weighted average method as being appropriate for costing the inventory. This is because the units do not move first in, first out nor last in, first out, but in a random fashion.

First, compute the weighted average cost per unit:

Cost of Goods Available for Sale	Number of Units Available for Sale	Explanation
$500,000	800,000	Beginning inventory balance
90,000	100,000	Purchase transaction #1
50,000	50,000	Purchase transaction #8
$640,000	950,000 units	TOTALS

$640,000 ÷ 950,000 = $0.67 per unit approximately.

Then, calculate the Ending Inventory, based on the weighted average method:

Beginning Merchandise Inventory (Item A)		Purchases Of Merchandise (Item A)		Cost of Goods Available For Sale (Item A)		Ending Merchandise Inventory (Item A)		Cost of Goods Sold (Item A)
$500,000; 800,000 units	+	$140,000; 150,000 units	=	$640,000; 950,000 units available	–	$308,200; 460,000 @ $0.67	=	331,800

Yucan Ceramics Ltd.
Income Statement
For the month ended August 31, 2014

Sales Revenue		$672,000
Less: Cost of Goods Sold*		331,800
Gross Profit		340,200
Operating Expenses:		
Rent Expense	$23,500	
Salaries Expense	80,000	
Wages Expense	45,200	
Insurance Expense	5,250	
Depreciation Expense	1,400	
Miscellaneous Expense	15,800	
Total Operating Expenses		(171,150)
Realized Loss on Sale of Temporary Investments		(10,000)**
Total Expenses and Realized Loss		(181,150)
Income before Income Taxes		159,050
Income Tax Expense (40%)		(63,620)
Net Income		**$95,430**

*From Cost of Goods Sold Schedule.

**We will ignore the true tax treatment of this realized loss.

Yucan Ceramics Ltd.
Balance Sheet
As at August 31, 2014

ASSETS		$
Cash		265,700
Account Receivable		958,500
*Merchandise Inventory**		308,200
Prepaid Insurance		63,000
Equipment	$420,000	
Less: Accumulated Depreciation	(70,800)	349,200
TOTAL ASSETS		1,944,600
LIABILITIES		
Accounts Payable		378,300
Salaries Payable		80,000
Wages Payable		45,200
*Income Taxes Payable***		130,620
Total Liabilities		634,120
OWNERS' EQUITY		
Share Capital		250,000
*Retained Earnings****		1,060,480
Total Owners' Equity		1,310,480
TOTAL LIABILITIES AND OWNERS' EQUITY		**1,944,600**

**The inventory remaining on August 31, 2014 must be the Ending Inventory as per the Cost of Goods Sold Schedule.*

***Income Taxes Payable includes Income Tax Expense for July: $67,000 + $63,620 = $130,620.*

****$965,050 + $95,430 = $1,060,480.*

NOTE: *the change in inventory costing methods must appear as a note in the financial statements, along with the effect of the change on reported assets and income. For simplicity, we do not show it here.*

Part g) CLOSING ENTRIES:

First, the Adjusting Entry for Income Taxes:

Yucan Ceramics Ltd. – General Journal

August 31, 2014 - Transaction #16	$	$
Income Tax Expense	63,620	
Income Taxes Payable		63,620
To record the income tax expense for the month of August.		

Computation: *obtained from the Income Statement.*

Next, all the Closing Entries:

Yucan Ceramics Ltd. – General Journal – Closing Entries

August 31, 2014	$	$
Sales Revenue	672,000	
Income Summary		672,000
To close Sales Revenue to Income Summary.		

August 31, 2014	$	$
Income Summary	500,000	
Merchandise Inventory		500,000
To transfer the beginning inventory balance to Income Summary.		

August 31, 2014	$	$
Income Summary	140,000	
Purchases		140,000
To transfer the Purchases balance to Income Summary.		

August 31, 2014	$	$
Merchandise Inventory	308,200	
Income Summary		308,200
To transfer the ending inventory balance to Income Summary and account for Cost of Goods Sold through Income Summary.		

August 31, 2014	$	$
Income Summary	23,500	
Rent Expense		23,500
To close the Rent Expense to Income Summary.		

August 31, 2014	$	$
Income Summary	80,000	
Salaries Expense		80,000
To close the Salaries Expense to Income Summary.		

August 31, 2014	$	$
Income Summary	45,200	
Wages Expense		45,200
To close the Wages Expense to Income Summary.		

August 31, 2014	$	$
Income Summary	5,250	
Insurance Expense		5,250
To close the Insurance Expense to Income Summary.		

August 31, 2014	$	$
Income Summary	1,400	
Depreciation Expense		1,400
To close the Depreciation Expense to Income Summary.		

August 31, 2014	$	$
Income Summary	15,800	
Miscellaneous Expense		15,800
To close the Miscellaneous Expense to Income Summary.		

August 31, 2014	$	$
Income Summary	10,000	
Realized Loss on Sale of Temporary Investments		10,000
To close the Realized Loss on Sale of Temporary Investments to Income Summary.		

August, 2014	$	$
Income Summary	63,620	
Income Tax Expense		63,620
To close the Income Tax Expense to Income Summary.		

August, 2014	$	$
Income Summary	95,430	
Retained Earnings		95,430
To close the Income Summary to Retained Earnings.		

Posting Ledger: The first balances are shown from the Adjusted Trial Balance.

Cash	
Bal. 265,700	

Accounts Receivable	
Bal. 958,500	

Merchandise Inventory	
Bal. 500,000	500,000 close
End 308,200	
Bal. 308,200	

Prepaid Insurance	
Bal. 63,000	

Equipment	
Bal. 420,000	

Accumulated Depreciation	
	70,800 Bal.

Accounts Payable	
	378,300 Bal.

Salaries Payable	
	80,000 Bal.

Wages Payable	
	45,200 Bal.

Income Taxes Payable	
	67,000 Bal.
	63,620 (adjusting)
	130,620 Bal.

Share Capital	
	250,000 Bal.

Retained Earnings	
	965,050 Bal.
	95,430 (closing)
	1,060,480 Bal.

Sales Revenue	
close 672,000	672,000 Bal.

Purchases	
Bal. 140,000	140,000 close

Rent Expense	
Bal. 23,500	23,500 close

Salaries Expense	
Bal. 80,000	80,000 close

Wages Expense	
Bal. 45,200	45,200 close

Insurance Expense	
Bal. 5,250	5,250 close

Depreciation Expense	
Bal. 1,400	1,400 close

Miscellaneous Expense	
Bal. 15,800	15,800 close

Realized Loss on Sale of Temporary Investments	
Bal. 10,000	10,000 close

Income Tax Expense	
adjust. 63,620	63,620 close

Income Summary			
		672,000	Sales
Beginning Inventory	500,000	308,200	Ending Inventory
Purchases	140,000		

Note: the difference here is Gross Profit of $340,200!

Rent	23,500		
Salaries	80,000		
Wages	45,200		
Insurance	5,250		
Depreciation	1,400		
Miscellaneous	15,800		
Realized loss	10,000		
Income Tax	63,620		
		95,430 Bal.	
Close	95,430	*Note: this is Net Income, we credit it to Retained Earnings.*	

Part h) POST-CLOSING TRIAL BALANCE:

Yucan Ceramics Ltd.
Post-Closing Trial Balance
As at August 31, 2014

Account	Debit $	Credit $
Cash	265,700	
Accounts Receivable	958,500	
Merchandise Inventory	308,200	
Prepaid Insurance	63,000	
Equipment	420,000	
Accumulated Depreciation		70,800
Accounts Payable		378,300
Salaries Payable		80,000
Wages Payable		45,200
Income Taxes Payable		130,620
Share Capital		250,000
Retained Earnings		1,060,480
TOTAL	2,015,400	2,015,400

Part i) INVENTORY QUESTION:

Yes and no. With the weighted average method the relationship between cost of goods sold and the number of units sold can be directly inferred. For example, Yucan Ceramics Ltd. has a weighted average cost of $0.67 per tile. In August, the cost of goods sold was $331,800. Therefore, $331,800 ÷ $0.67 = 495,224 (approximately) tiles have been accounted for as sold. However, we know from transaction #2 that only 480,000 tiles were sold. Thus, about 15,000 tiles have gone missing during the month of August. The difference of 224 tiles is part of the rounding error, a result of using the weighted average method.

In fact, the $0.67 per tile cost has been rounded from $0.67368421 to two decimal places. Using the more accurate eight decimal place figure reduces the number of missing tiles, but not substantially. The company still has an inventory management problem.

Although the weighted average method allows us to see this direct relationship, other inventory costing methods permit this indirectly. From Case One, using FIFO, we knew that 22,000 tiles were missing by simply completing the Cost of Goods Sold Schedule using units instead of dollars. Recall, there were 1,172,000 units available for sale. The case specifically told us 350,000 units were sold. The difference of 822,000 tiles should end up as inventory. When the physical units were counted at the end of July, only 800,000 tiles were there. Thus, 22,000 tiles were missing.

Clearly, Yucan Ceramics Ltd. has an inventory management problem. Each month a substantial number of tiles disappear. In August this amounted to $10,050 (15,000 x $0.67 = $10,050). The best way to increase control is by changing the inventory system from periodic to perpetual. As the ending inventory balance will then be known at any date during the month, interim physical counts will reveal exactly when the tiles are disappearing, if the new system functions properly. All employees will be aware of the greater control over inventory.

To the extent feasible, the costing method chosen should be based on the physical flow of goods. In this case the change to the weighted average method is an improvement since the movement of tiles is random and does not follow FIFO, LIFO or Specific Identification.

Notes

Chapter Four - The Amortization of Capital Assets

The Reason for This Chapter

This chapter provides an in-depth discussion on Capital Assets. We distinguish these assets from current assets by considering their expected life. Companies count on using their capital assets for a long period of time.

Capital assets usually represent a sizeable investment for any company. We must give special consideration to how the cost of using these assets matches the revenues they produce. Up to this point, the books in this series have only examined the accounting treatment of physical assets. In addition, only one depreciation technique was specified: the straight-line method.

In this chapter we account for the cost of using long-term assets through a process known as amortization. This allows for alternative methods of calculating depreciation. We introduce intangible assets along with a variety of ways to account for their use.

What Do You Already Know?

Pre-Test

Question One

On January 1, 2014, Michealmas Corporation purchased a machine for $89,000. The production manager had estimated it could last for 25 years, if used part-time. The plant manager has decided to run the machine full-time for 15 years and then dispose of it for $3,500. Prepare the journal entries needed to report the acquisition and first month's depreciation. Use the straight-line method to complete the spaces provided below:

Date:	**Debit**	**Credit**

Date:	**Debit**	**Credit**

Computation:

Question Two

At what value will Michealmas Corporation carry the machinery on the January 31, 2014 balance sheet?

Answers to the Pre-test

Answer to Question One

Date: *January 1, 2014*	**Debit**	**Credit**
Machinery	*$89,000*	
Cash		*$89,000*
To record the purchase of a machine for $89,000.		

Date: January 31, 2014	*Debit*	*Credit*
Depreciation Expense	$475	
Accumulated Depreciation		$475
To record depreciation expense on the machine for the month of January 2014.		

Computation:

($89,000 - $3,500) ÷ 15 = $5,700 per year

$5,700 ÷ 12 = $475 per month

Note: *The depreciation charge should reflect the expense of using the machine for a specific period. Since the plant manager has directed the machine be used full-time for 15 years, that becomes the basis for computing the expense.*

Answer to Question Two

The carrying value of the machinery will be at its acquisition cost less any accumulated depreciation. On January 31, 2014, the balance sheet will show:

Machinery, at cost	$89,000
Less: accumulated depreciation	475
Carrying Value	$88,525

We often refer to the carrying value as the book value, or net book value.

How This Chapter Relates to Other Chapters in This Book

We classify the assets on the balance sheet according to the length of time we expect they will be available for use. Chapters One and Two examined current assets and detailed the particulars behind calculating the carrying values of those assets.

Capital assets must also be carried on the balance sheet. How we use them affects their value. While many methods of amortization exist, the appropriateness of each technique must often be determined by particular circumstances. This chapter considers how to carry capital assets.

This book addresses accounting for carrying values. Chapter Five concludes the discussion with a look at how we carry liabilities on the balance sheet. Chapter Six provides a review.

What Are the Topics in This Chapter?

Grouping accounts according to their life expectancy provides users of financial statements with two benefits: 1) additional information - they now have some idea as to the age of each account and 2) clarity - it becomes easy to see at a glance which accounts are the youngest or oldest.

In this chapter we look at how to carry capital assets. Because management expects to use these assets for a long period of time, they form the latter part of the asset section on the balance sheet.

Topics Covered in Chapter Four	*Level of Importance*
What Are Capital Assets?	
Definition	***
Plant Assets	***
Natural Resources	**
Intangible Assets	**
What Is Amortization?	
Depreciation	***
Appreciation	**
Acquiring Capital Assets	
The Cost Principle, Again	***
Capitalization	**

Topics Covered in Chapter Four	*Level of Importance*
Carrying Capital Assets	
Calculating the Cost of Use	***
Problems in Estimating Usage Costs	**
Typical Cost Patterns	**
Depreciating Capital Assets	
The Straight-line Method	***
The Declining-balance Method	***
Productive-output Method	***
Combining Methods	**
Other Issues in Depreciation	
Repairs and Maintenance	**
Improvements	**
Depleting Capital Assets	
The Depletion Rate	**
Amortizing Intangible Capital Assets	
Without Future Benefits	**
With Future Benefits	**
Intangible Assets with Future Benefits	*
Disposing of Capital Assets	
Gains and Losses	***

Legend

*	indicates a low level of importance
**	indicates a medium level of importance
***	indicates a high level of importance

What Are Capital Assets?

Definition

Accountants classify those assets expected to be in use for a long time as capital or fixed assets. That is, they are not current assets. Using that definition, a long time is more than the greater of one year and the operating cycle.

Capital assets can be tangible or intangible. Tangible assets physically exist - you can touch them. Most of a company's assets are tangible, like inventory and machinery. In practice, however, the term "tangible assets" normally refers to *long-term* physical assets that are *not held for re-sale*. Examples include buildings, equipment, trucks, and the aforementioned machinery. Intangible assets are not generally discernable by touch. They are legal rights that have monetary implications. Examples are patents and copyrights.

We classify tangible assets as either current or capital, depending on their expected life. As legal rights tend to exist for periods longer than one year, we report intangibles as capital assets.

Tangible capital assets may be further classified as Plant or Natural Resources. Plant assets include the equipment and machinery needed in the production process. We find these capital assets inside the business location - they are in the plant. Natural resources are long-term assets existing in nature. They are outside. Iron ore that must be mined or trees that must be cut both fall into this category.

In this chapter we divide capital assets into three groups: Plant, Natural Resources and Intangibles.

What Is Amortization?

In order to capture the cost of using a capital asset during a specific period, we must find some way to determine that cost.

Amortization is a process of allocating a portion of the asset's acquisition cost as an expense in the current accounting period. This concept is familiar to you.

When a company expects to reap the benefits of carrying its assets within the current period, the process of capturing these periodic costs is relatively simple. You already know how to amortize current assets through the adjusting entry process. For example, you would take the total cost of insurance, prepaid for one year and simply split it into twelve equal portions. You then report each portion as the insurance expense for that month.

When a company anticipates the benefits of using an asset will last a long time, the allocation process becomes more complicated. However, you know something about this too. You are familiar with the Straight-line method of depreciating capital assets. Let's examine the concept of depreciation and then compare it to appreciation.

Depreciation

When the value of a capital asset declines, we may say it has depreciated. After using an asset repeatedly over time to generate revenues, we naturally expect its value to decline. The matching principle dictates accounting must attempt to capture this cost of usage and report it in the appropriate accounting period. While many different methods provide assistance in measuring this cost, we examine only a few in this chapter.

We use the term "depreciation" to specifically describe the amortization of plant assets. We say natural resources are "depleted". When we allocate a portion of an intangible asset as a cost, we say it has been "amortized". In each case there is one common idea: each period, we attempt to allocate the cost of using a capital asset in that period.

Appreciation

Some assets appreciate in value. Should we report this gain? Probably not. Recall from chapter One our discussion of Temporary

Investments. There, we highlighted the philosophy behind good accounting: be conservative in what we report. What goes up in value, may come down. So, we report both realized and unrealized losses but only realized gains.

The main difference between appreciation and the amortization process is control. Appreciation of assets is not usually under control of the business. For example, the value of a building owned by a company may rise. Such an increase has more to do with real estate conditions than with the business itself. It just happened. You may compare it to the value of a Temporary Investment rising. It is a windfall and not a result of the operating process. We should not report the increase until it becomes certain; we recognize gains only when they are realized, i.e., when the underlying asset is sold.

Amortization occurs because management has directed an asset be used in the operating process to help generate revenues. Recording and reporting amortization is an attempt to allocate to specific accounting periods, the cost of using (consuming) the asset.

Some assets are not expected to decline in value, even when they are used in the operating process. In fact, their value regularly increases with age. Commonly, the capital assets we expect will appreciate in value are land, art and antiques. We also expect the value of long-term investments in securities to rise. While we report any gains when realized, we do not attempt to amortize these assets unless the operating process reduces their value.

Acquiring Capital Assets

The Cost Principle, Again

We report newly acquired capital assets at their acquisition cost. According to the cost principle, this includes any costs needed to obtain the asset and get it into working order. Therefore, the acquisition cost is not limited to the purchase price of the asset itself. It commonly includes any shipping and installation costs as well as legal fees, engineering or set-up charges and tax costs. Under certain conditions even profits lost as a result of the capital asset purchase, may be included. For simplicity, we will adhere to the most common costs in this chapter.

Capitalization

When the acquisition cost includes costs incurred to get the asset ready for its intended use we say we are capitalizing these costs. What is the alternative? To report them directly on the income statement as expenses, but that would not be appropriate because these costs provide us with benefits which extend beyond the current accounting period.

In other words, accountants do not have the freedom to choose. The Cost Principle clearly states the acquisition cost of an asset includes all costs needed to get it up and running (operating) for its intended use. Often many costs other than the invoice cost of the asset must be incurred. Accountants tie these other costs with the asset purchase price in determining the acquisition cost. Capitalization is the process of including these costs together. Since we amortize the entire acquisition cost, we may say these other costs have been capitalized.

Now You Try It

Learning Exercise One

Applejacks Ltd. purchased a machine for $25,000; the machine will be used in the company's operating process. In addition to the purchase price, there was 5% sales tax which is not recoverable. To get the machine in working order, a consulting engineer was hired for $2,000. Several laborers worked to install the machine at a cost of $750. In order to ensure it worked properly, a test run was made at a cost of $1,500. The bookkeeper decided to spend the day watching the set-up. His daily wage was $120. Assume all of the preceding costs were paid with cash. What is the acquisition cost of this machine?

Answers

Answer to Learning Exercise One

The cost of the bookkeeper should not be included, as he was not needed to get this machine running. In fact, he wasted $120 of the company's money by not performing his work that day. All the other costs are included:

Cost of machine	*$25,000*
Sales tax (5%)	*1,250*
Consulting Engineer	*2,000*
Labor	*750*
Test-run	*1,500*
Acquisition Cost	***$30,500***

Carrying Capital Assets

Calculating the Cost of Use

We carry non-current assets at their book value. That is, the acquisition cost less any amortization charges. Thus, at any given time, the book value approximately represents the value of the asset that has not yet been consumed (used up). Often, however, this is only a very rough approximation of the asset's real value. The real, or market, value of the asset is generally only known if a formal, e.g., independent, appraisal is performed.

Choosing the method that best represents how the asset is used over time can be tricky. Several problems arise in calculating the amortization charge, or cost of usage. We examine the potential problems with estimating the usage charge next.

Problems in Estimating Usage Costs

While many factors lead to the eventual retirement of assets, the main reasons can be described as either 1) wear and tear or 2) obsolescence. In other words, assets become worn out from use and because newer and better versions become available. Understanding why the value of an asset deteriorates is helpful in determining how we measure this cost.

Three estimation problems arise in allocating amortization costs. First, we must determine the "depreciable" cost of the asset. This is not simply the acquisition cost. In determining the depreciable cost we must also consider an estimate of any value expected to be received (or additional cost to be incurred) upon the eventual disposal of the asset. That gives rise to a second forecast; an estimation of its service life - how long the company expects to keep the asset in use. The third problem concerns estimating the cost pattern while the asset is in use.

The estimated disposal value can be either positive or negative. It depends on what the company plans to do with the asset after it has finished using it. A negative disposal value occurs when management expects it must pay to have the asset taken away. A positive value comes about when it believes someone will buy the asset once its service life is over.

The estimated service life must consider how long the asset could be used and when it will become obsolete. Taken together, management thus determines the length of time it expects to use the asset. This is one of the most difficult tasks in the amortization process.

To estimate service life correctly, management must be able to foresee the creation of new products not in its line of business. For this reason most service life estimates are incorrect. Accounting must be flexible on this point. Thus, estimates of service life are often reconsidered every few years. While we do not expect you to estimate either the service life or disposal value in this chapter, we do require you to revise depreciation calculations once these estimates change.

Now You Try It

Learning Exercise Two

An office machine was purchased on January 1, 2009 for $9,200. At that time, it was estimated the machine would operate for fifteen years and then be disposed of for $200. The straight-line method was deemed appropriate.

In the beginning of 2014, it was realized that the machine would probably last only a total of ten years, but it could still be disposed of for $200 at that time. What annual depreciation expense was taken in the first five years of operation? What annual depreciation expense should be taken in the year 2014?

Answers

Answer to Learning Exercise Two

For the first five years of operation the annual depreciation expense is:
($9,200 - $200) ÷ 15 years = $600 per year.

Therefore, with five years of depreciation taken, the accumulated depreciation balance will be: 5 years x $600 = $3,000.

The amount of depreciation not yet taken equals the carrying value of the asset:
$9,200 - $3,000 = $6,200.

Therefore, the revised annual depreciation charge beginning in 2014 is:
($6,200 - $200) ÷ (10 years - 5 years) = $1,200 per year.

The estimated cost pattern should reflect how the asset is used up over time. We examine typical cost patterns, next.

Typical Cost Patterns

Since assets may be used in a variety of ways, many different cost patterns exist to reflect specific usage. They fall within the range of immediate write-off to no amortization whatsoever. For example, if an asset's value is completely diminished the very first time it is used, its cost pattern must allow for expensing the full acquisition price immediately. At the opposite extreme, if the asset will never decline in value, then the cost pattern reflects this and zero amortization is taken. Land is such an asset.

Most assets are not fully used up on day one, nor never used up. Therefore, most cost patterns fall within these two extremes. Three general patterns exist: accelerated, constant or decelerated.

Accelerated means most of the cost happens quickly. We speed up the expensing of the asset. That is, the value of the asset declines rapidly during the early years of its service life. Thus, the amortization expense will be greatest in the first accounting period and then decline each subsequent period.

Constant refers to a pattern where the usage cost is the same in each period of the asset's life. This is a method you know. We call it Straight-line depreciation. The depreciation expense is the same each time we report it.

Decelerated is the opposite of accelerated - the recognition of costs are slowed down. The usage cost will be smallest in the first period and rise with each additional period. As we rarely see this pattern in financial accounting, we will not demonstrate it.

Typically, the cost of using capital assets tends to follow either an accelerated or constant pattern, or a mix of the two. Sometimes none of these patterns is followed. The amortization pattern may also be based on activity, such as, how many units are being produced. We highlight the cost pattern assumption behind each commonly used depreciation method, next.

Depreciating Capital Assets

The Straight-line Method

So far, we have used this method exclusively in this series of books. Your familiarity with it will enhance your understanding of the other methods. The Straight-line method assumes the cost pattern is constant. Thus, the depreciation expense is the same for each period during the asset's service life. We reviewed this technique in the Pre-Test as well as in Learning Exercise Two.

The Declining-balance Method

This method assumes an accelerated cost pattern. That is, the depreciation expense will be greatest in the first period and become smaller and smaller in each passing period. The Declining-balance method assumes the rate of decline is constant. This means the dollar value of the depreciation declines each period, but the rate of change is constant.

At the end of the asset's service life it is unlikely the carrying value will equal its disposal cost with this method. Therefore, we do not adjust the acquisition cost, by the disposal value. Instead, we can anticipate the problem and adjust the depreciation expense in one or more of the later years. For simplicity, in this chapter we will simply adjust the last year for any difference needed. Just prior to disposing of the asset, its carrying value will equal its disposal cost.

Now You Try It

Learning Exercise Three

At the beginning of this year, Elf Toys Corporation purchased a new machine to be used in its production process. The invoice price was $60,000. There was $4,000 in set-up costs. Management estimates the machine will be used for four years, after which time it will be sold for $5,000. Furthermore, it believes the machine's value will decline at a constant rate of 40% each year. Calculate the annual depreciation expense, accumulated depreciation, carrying value and any end of life adjustments needed for this machine. Complete the table provided below.

Start of Year	Acquisition Cost (1)	Accumulated Depreciation (2)	Carrying Value (1) - (2) = (3)	Depreciation Rate (4)	Annual Depreciation Expense (3) x (4) = (5)
1	$64,000			40%	
2	64,000			40%	
3	64,000			40%	
4	64,000			40%	
End of Year 4	64,000		5,000	Adjustment	*

*Computation:

Answers

Answer to Learning Exercise Three

Start of Year	Acquisition Cost (1)	Accumulated Depreciation (2)	Carrying Value (1) - (2) = (3)	Depreciation Rate (4)	Annual Depreciation Expense (3) x (4) = (5)
1	$64,000	$ 0	$64,000	40%	$25,600
2	64,000	25,600	38,400	40%	15,360
3	64,000	40,960	23,040	40%	9,216
4	64,000	50,176	13,824	40%	5,529.60
End of Year 4	64,000	55,705.60	5,000	Adjustment	3,294.40*

**Note: at the end of its service life the carrying value should be equal to the disposal value. Under the Declining-balance Method we may adjust the last year's depreciation expense to include this difference. For Elf Toys, the carrying value of this machine should equal its disposal value of $5,000 at the end of year four, assuming this is still an appropriate value. However, the unadjusted carrying value is $8,294.40 at the end of year 4, i.e., $64,000 - $55,705.60. To resolve the problem we increase the year four depreciation expense by $3,294.40, i.e., $8,294.40 - $5,000.*

For the new machine owned by Elf Toys, notice how the depreciation expense declines each year. This accelerated cost pattern reflects the speeding up of depreciation. The largest usage cost occurs in the earliest period.

Productive-output Method

For some assets we base the cost usage pattern on activity. While the idea is straightforward, it presents a new estimation problem. If the service life of the asset depends on its total productive capacity then we must estimate how many units (or other measurable output) it can produce. We calculate the depreciation expense according to how much we use the asset each period.

Such assets are limited to producing a certain number of units, or output. Therefore, the cost pattern does not either accelerate or remain constant with time. Rather, it is completely dependent on how actively the machine is used. Once the total output is achieved, the service life of the machine has expired.

With the productive-output method we first determine the depreciation cost per unit of activity. This is based on the total output expected from the asset. We compute the depreciation cost per unit as:

(acquisition cost less disposal value) ÷ estimated number of units (or output)

We then compute the depreciation expense as:

depreciation cost per unit x the number of units (output) produced

Now You Try it

Learning Exercise Four

Let's revisit the Elf Toys Corporation. The production manager estimates the new $64,000 machine can produce a total of 100,000 units. Therefore, its life may not be limited to four years, nor is the depreciation based on the 40% constant usage rate. The estimated disposal value is $5,000. The sales manager estimates that he can sell the toy this machine produces as follows:

Year	Estimated Number of Units Sold
1	25,000
2	10,000
3	35,000
4	10,000
5	20,000

The company will produce the units to be sold in the year of the estimated sale. Calculate the annual depreciation expense, accumulated depreciation and carrying value for this machine. You must first compute the depreciation cost per unit.

Complete the table provided below.

Computation:

Start of Year	Acquisition Cost (1)	Accumulated Depreciation (2)	Carrying Value (1) - (2) = (3)	Units Produced (4)	Depreciation Cost per Rate	Annual Depreciation Expense (4) x (5) = (6)
1						
2						
3						
4						
5						
End of Year 5						

Answers

Answer to Learning Exercise Four

Computation:

Depreciation cost per unit
= ($64,000 - $5,000) ÷ 100,000
= $0.59 per unit

Start of Year	*Acquisition Cost (1)*	*Accumulated Depreciation (2)*	*Carrying Value (1) - (2) = (3)*	*Units Produced (4)*	*Depreciation Cost per Rate*	*Annual Depreciation Expense (4) x (5) = (6)*
1	$64,000	$ 0	$64,000	25,000	$0.59	$14,750
2	64,000	14,750	49,250	10,000	$0.59	5,900
3	64,000	20,650	43,350	35,000	$0.59	20,650
4	64,000	41,300	22,700	10,000	$0.59	5,900
5	64,000	47,200	16,800	20,000	$0.59	11,800
End of Year 5	64,000	59,000	5,000	100,000		

At the end of year five the acquisition cost less the accumulated depreciation equals the carrying value. This must be the same as the disposal value, assuming this is still an appropriate value. That is: $64,000 - $59,000 = $5,000. No adjustments are needed for the productive-output method unless the estimate of the total units produced is revised or the estimated disposal value changes. For simplicity, we will ignore those possibilities.

Combining Methods

In many jurisdictions, a combination of depreciation methods occurs. This is the case in the United States. For tax purposes, American companies compute depreciation charges according to MACRS (Modified Accelerated Cost Recovery System). Under this system assets are grouped in various classes. Depreciation calculations generally follow the declining-balance method, but the straight-line method must be used for certain types of assets. In this way no ad-hoc adjustments (like the one we saw in Learning

Exercise Three) are needed. The government assigns the usage rates and service lives needed for each asset class.

Because depreciation is a tax-deductible expense, the depreciation charge claimed reduces the amount of taxes a company must pay. There is a natural incentive to overstate the depreciation expense in any given tax year. Therefore, governments are inclined to exercise control over depreciation claims. As in the United States, the national government of most countries dictates the depreciation method used by companies for income tax purposes.

Other Issues in Depreciation

Repairs and Maintenance

One consequence of using depreciable assets will be maintenance and repairs. These expenses are usually nominal in value, compared to the acquisition cost of the asset. They are required to insure the asset will function properly throughout its service life. They do not significantly improve the life or value of the asset - they simply maintain it in accordance with its intended use. Thus, repairs are generally of a minor, or routine, nature.

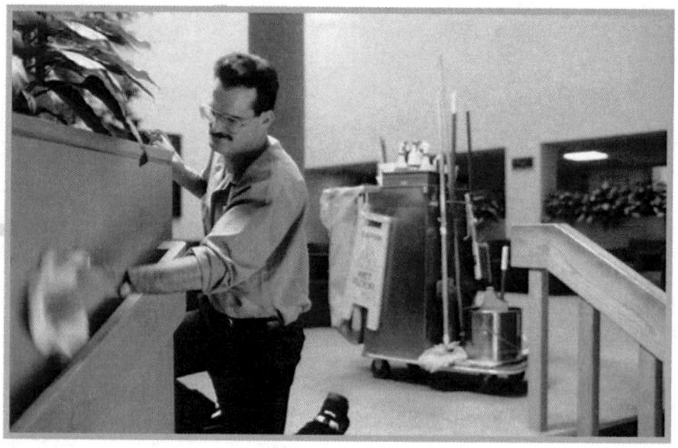

Maintenance and repairs often occur according to some timetable. We treat them as a regular operating expense by reporting the amount directly on the income statement. Since we do not capitalize these transactions they have no effect on the balance sheet, except of course, to reduce cash and owners' equity or increase payables.

Now You Try It

Learning Exercise Five

Keller's Katerers has several delivery trucks. The fleet manager regularly schedules maintenance visits for each vehicle. On July 15, 2014 the bookkeeper for Keller's Katerers issues a check to satisfy the regularly scheduled maintenance visit for three trucks. Included in the invoice were minor repairs. The invoice amount was $1,200. Prepare the journal entry.

Date	Debit	Credit

Answers

Answer to Learning Exercise Five

Date July 15, 2014	*Debit*	*Credit*
Repairs and maintenance	$1,200	
Cash		$1,200
To record the repairs and maintenance on three delivery trucks.		

Improvements

Betterments or improvements are major events. Relatively speaking, their cost is much higher than repairs and maintenance. Consequently, improvements *significantly* increase the service life or disposal value of the asset, or both.

Because they affect the asset value, we capitalize improvements on the balance sheet. Thus, the periodic depreciation charge for the asset will change. It must be recalculated to reflect the change in the asset's value or extension of its service life.

Now You Try It

Learning Exercise Six

On January 1, 2013, Chappers Inc. purchased some equipment that cost $200,000. At the time of purchase its estimated service life was 25 years with no disposal value. At the beginning of 2014, the following expenditures relating to the equipment took place:

Minor repairs	$ 5,000
Improvements	$50,000

The improvements will extend the service life of the equipment by 5 years. What was the annual depreciation charge for 2013? What will it be for 2014? Hint: this is a little tricky because you must adjust carrying value. Refer back to Learning Exercise Two.

Answers

Answer to Learning Exercise Six

In 2013, prior to the improvements, the annual depreciation charge was:

($200,000 - $0) ÷ 25 years = $8,000 per year.

After one year the company has already claimed $8,000 of accumulated depreciation. Only the undepreciated portion of the asset is affected by the improvement. Therefore:

Cost of asset when acquired	*$ 200,000*
Less: accumulated depreciation	*(8,000)*
Undepreciated balance	*192,000*
Plus: Cost of improvement	*50,000*
Balance to be depreciated	***$ 242,000***

$242,000 ÷ (24 years remaining (per original estimate) + 5 years' extension) = new annual depreciation charge.
$242,000 ÷ 29 years = $8,344.83, rounded up to $8,345.
Therefore, beginning in 2014 the annual depreciation charge will be $8,345 for this equipment.

Depleting Capital Assets

The Depletion Rate

Like plant assets, natural resources decline in value as they are used up. Unlike plant assets, we deplete rather than depreciate natural resources.

We calculate a depletion rate based on the acquisition cost of the natural resource (less any estimated residual value, or plus any disposal costs) and the total number of units (or other measure of output), which we estimate the resource will yield. We compute the periodic depletion expense by multiplying the number of units withdrawn (extracted, etc.) during the period by the depletion rate. Thus, depletion is based on activity. Depletion is calculated in accordance with the productive-output method studied previously.

Whenever amortization is based on activity, an estimation problem results. It is difficult to forecast how many units a natural resource will actually provide. As time goes by, estimates become more reliable and the depletion rate will probably be changed. We adjust for depletion revisions in the same manner as those for depreciation.

Now You Try It

Learning Exercise Seven

On January 1, 2014, a large wooded lot was purchased for $56,000. In order to log the property, a road was built at a cost of $23,000. It is estimated the lot will yield 35,000 trees. The residual value of the land is estimated to be $17,000. 7,000 trees are harvested in the first year. What adjusting entry must be made on December 31, 2014, the end of the annual accounting period, to report the depletion? Show the adjusting entry in the space provided below:

Date	Debit	Credit

Computation:

Answers

Answer to Learning Exercise Seven

Date *December 31, 2014*	*Debit*	*Credit*
Depletion Expense	*$12,390*	
Land (wooded lot)		*$12,390*
To record the depletion of trees from the wooded lot.		

Computation:
The depletion rate is: ($56,000 + $23,000 - $17,000) ÷ 35,000 trees = $1.77 per tree.
By the year-end 7,000 trees are harvested: 7,000 x $1.77 = $12,390.

While many other complications arise in accounting for natural resources, we conclude our discussion here. We examine amortization of intangible assets next.

Amortizing Intangible Capital Assets

Assets without a physical form that will provide future benefits are considered to be intangible capital assets. We classify research and advertising costs along with trade secrets, patents, copyrights and many others as intangible capital assets. We must first decide if: 1) the costs incurred to obtain intangible assets will have quantifiable future benefits and can therefore be amortized or 2) no future benefits can be reasonably estimated. We examine each issue next.

Without Future Benefits

Intangible capital assets acquired at a cost may not provide future benefits that can be quantified, or reasonably estimated. In this case, the cost pattern follows the first extreme: expense the full amount of the cost immediately. In such a case, amortization is not appropriate because no future benefits (with which to match costs) can be reasonably estimated. The prevailing school of thought dictates that while these costs are incurred to achieve some future benefit, it is too difficult to quantify. Conservatism suggests it is better to write them off immediately rather than take an uneducated guess.

The Organization Expense studied in Chapter One of Volume One is an excellent example of an intangible capital asset without future benefits. Clearly, there are benefits to forming a corporation. Yet it is difficult to estimate exact dollar amounts. Therefore, it is better to immediately expense these costs. Another example is the research costs arising from scientific pursuits. Often these investigations are directed towards the pursuit of *general* knowledge and not a specific product. Therefore, we commonly expense these costs immediately.

With Future Benefits

When future benefits can be quantified, the next challenge is to decide how to amortize the acquisition cost once it has been capitalized. Justification of an appropriate cost pattern can always be debated. Historically, the practice of amortizing intangible capital assets has varied widely. Accounting Standards Boards revisit and debate this topic often.

Generally, tradition dictates how certain costs should be amortized. Because estimates of the benefits associated with intangibles are so unreliable, uniform practice among companies is probably more important over the long run, than the logic behind such decisions. Most intangibles are amortized using the straight-line method. In mainstream accounting, there is generally a 40-year limit on the amortization period used for individual intangible assets. Of course, attempts to justify specific transactions continuously evolve. Further discussion of this topic is beyond the scope of this book. Instead, we simply list and define the intangible capital assets that are commonly capitalized and amortized.

Intangible Assets with Future Benefits

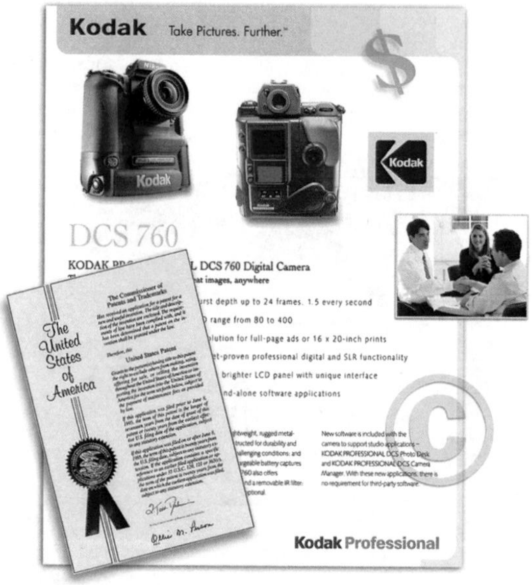

Advertising Costs: money spent towards promoting products with the goal of increasing sales.
Brand Names: product names that are legally registered and widely recognized. They generally provide higher sales.
Copyrights: exclusive legal rights given by an author or artist.
Development Costs: research findings directed toward developing a specific product. (However, in practice, development costs are usually not capitalized because the benefits are often very difficult to measure.)
Goodwill: the value of a firm in excess of its assets less liabilities. May be attributed to the entrepreneurial spirit of the company.
Patents: an exclusive legal right given to the inventor of a product or process that forbids others from making, or copying it.

Disposal of Capital Assets

When it is no longer desirable to hold a capital asset, the business disposes of it. Sometimes disposal is involuntary, such as in a fire or accident. Regardless, once the asset has been disposed of it must be removed from the balance sheet and all relevant accounts must be adjusted.

Gains and Losses

It is unlikely a company will dispose of assets at the carrying value. Therefore, at the time of disposal a gain or loss normally arises. Generally, two entries are made at this time: 1) to update the depreciation expense and accumulated depreciation to the date of disposal and 2) to record the gain or loss associated with the disposal.

Now You Try It

Learning Exercise Eight

The records of Smithson Inc. showed the following information pertaining to a piece of equipment on December 31, 2013:

Acquisition cost of equipment	$52,000
Accumulated depreciation	28,000

Depreciation had been calculated on a straight-line basis. The residual value of the equipment was estimated to be $3,000 and the estimated useful life was seven years in total.

At the beginning of April 2014, the equipment was sold for $26,000 cash. The company uses the calendar year for reporting purposes. How old was the equipment on January 1, 2014? Provide the journal entries related to the disposal of the equipment in the space provided.

First determine the annual depreciation expense:

Then use that information to determine the age of the equipment as at January 1, 2014:

Next, record the depreciation expense to the date of sale:

Date	Debit	Credit

Computation:

Now, compute the gain or loss on disposal and record it along with the disposal:

Date	Debit	Credit

Computations:

Answers

Answer to Learning Exercise Eight

To determine the age of the equipment on January 1, 2014, you must first determine the annual depreciation expense:

($52,000 - $3,000) ÷ 7 years = $7,000 per year.

Since there is $28,000 of accumulated depreciation as at January 1, 2014, the asset must be four years old on January 1, 2014 ($28,000 ÷ $7,000 = 4).

Since the asset is disposed of in early April, three months of depreciation should be expensed for the year 2014:

Date April 1, 2014	**Debit**	**Credit**
Depreciation Expense	$1,750	
Accumulated Depreciation		$1,750
To record the depreciation expense for the first 3 months of 2014.		

Computation:

$7,000 x 3 / 12 months = $1,750 for three months.

Now, the gain or loss on disposal must be computed and recorded along with the disposal:

Date April 1, 2014	**Debit**	**Credit**
Cash	$26,000	
Accumulated Depreciation	$29,750*	
Gain on Disposal of Equipment		$ 3,750**
Equipment		$52,000
To record the disposal of equipment.		

Computations:

**$28,000 + $1,750 = $29,750*

***$52,000 - $29,750 = $22,250 (the carrying value of the equipment on April 1, 2014).*

Because the equipment was sold at a price greater than its carrying value, there is a gain on disposal, namely: $26,000 - $22,250 = $3,750 gain.

What You Have Learned in This Chapter

In this chapter we explored how to carry capital assets. We accounted for their acquisition, amortization and disposition. We looked at both tangible and intangible assets as well as grouping them into Plant, Natural Resources or Intangibles on the balance sheet.

While many methods of amortization are available, we examined only a few. We studied three typical cost patterns as well as a depreciation method for each. That is, the declining-balance method assumes an accelerated cost pattern, the straight-line method assumes a constant cost pattern and the productive-output method uses an activity-based cost pattern.

Reviewing the section "Important Terms in this Chapter" provides a great summary. It serves to test your understanding. If you can define all these terms, you most likely have a good grasp of the topics covered. You will further test this knowledge by completing the Self-Test and Practice Problems. Good Luck.

Important Terms in This Chapter

Accelerate: speed up.

Acquisition Cost: includes all the costs associated with getting the asset into working order.

Allocation: assignment. Depreciation is a process of allocating or assigning costs.

Amortization: the general process of charging off amounts by installments. Depreciation is an example of amortization. Also, the specific process of allocating the periodic cost of using an intangible asset during an accounting period

Capital Assets: also known as fixed or noncurrent assets. Those assets expected to be in use for a long period of time; longer than the greater of the operating cycle or one-year.

Capitalization: the process of including necessary expenditures with the asset purchase price to determine the acquisition cost. As the entire acquisition cost is amortized, we say these expenditures have been capitalized.

Cost Pattern: how the asset will be used up over time. Six general patterns are: immediate, accelerated, constant, decelerated, zero or activity-based.

Decelerate: slow down.

Declining Balance Method: accelerated cost pattern following a constant usage rate. Depreciation expense becomes smaller each subsequent period of the asset's service life.

Depletion: the process of allocating the periodic cost of using a natural resource to the specific accounting periods which benefit from the use of those assets.

Depletion Rate: acquisition cost of the resource less estimated disposal value (or plus estimated disposal costs) divided by the total estimated available units or other appropriate measure of output.

Depreciation: the process of allocating the periodic cost of using long-term plant assets (or other depreciable tangible assets) to the specific accounting periods which benefit from the use of those assets.

Depreciation Cost per Unit: acquisition cost less estimated disposal value (or plus estimated disposal costs) divided by the total estimated available units (or other appropriate measure of output).

Disposal value: also known as salvage or residual value. The expected value of the asset once its service life is complete. If this value is negative, e.g., dismantling costs, we often refer to this amount as disposal costs.

Improvements: also known as betterments. Major changes made to an asset resulting in significantly increasing its value or service life. We capitalize improvements.

Intangible assets: are generally not discernable by touch. Legal rights like patents and copyrights are examples.

Natural resources: physically exist in nature and may be taken for use in the operating process. Copper and gold that can be mined or timberland that can be harvested are examples.

Obsolete: no longer in style. Growing old. An asset becomes obsolete as newer and better versions become available.

Productive-output Method: cost pattern is based on activity. Is dependent upon the total output of the asset and how it is used. One must compute the depreciation cost per unit (or other measure of output) in order to use this method.

Service Life: the length of time the asset will be in service, or use.

Straight-line Method: constant cost pattern. Depreciation expense is the same in each period of the asset's service life, unless the estimated service life, disposal value, etc. change.

Tangible assets: exist physically - you can touch them. Most of a company's assets are tangible - like inventory and machinery. In practice, the term "tangible assets" normally refers to long-term physical assets that are not held for re-sale. Examples include buildings, machinery and equipment, trucks, etc.

Should You Move on to the Next Chapter?

Self-Test for Chapter Four

Question One

What is amortization?

____

____

Question Two

What is capitalization?

Question Three

Describe three problems in determining amortization costs.

Question Four

A manufacturing machine was purchased on January 1, 2010 for $22,000. At that time, it was estimated the machine would operate for ten years and then be disposed of for $2,000. The straight-line method was deemed appropriate.

During year 2014, it was realized that the machine would probably last only six years in total, and that it would be disposed of for $1,000 at that time. What annual depreciation expense was taken in the first four years of operation? What annual depreciation expense should be taken in year 2014?

Question Five

Describe the three typical cost patterns found in financial accounting, and name a suitable depreciation method for each cost pattern.

Question Six

The records of Warrant Ltd. showed the following information pertaining to a piece of equipment on *October 31, 2013:*

Acquisition cost of equipment $165,000
Accumulated depreciation 58,000

Depreciation had been calculated on a straight-line basis. The residual value was estimated at $13,000 and the useful life of the equipment was estimated to be twelve years.

At the beginning of March 2014, the equipment was sold for $100,000 cash. The year ends *each October 31st*, for reporting purposes. Provide the journal entries related to the disposal of the equipment in the space provided below.

You must first determine the annual depreciation expense:

Next, record the depreciation expense to the date of sale:

Date	Debit	Credit

Computation:

Now, compute the gain or loss on disposal and record it along with the disposal:

Date	Debit	Credit

Computations:

Answers to Self-Test for Chapter Four

Answer to Question One

Amortization is a process of allocating a portion of the asset's acquisition cost as an expense in the current accounting period. This process is an important application of the matching principle; the estimated cost of consuming the asset ("using it up") is matched with the revenues derived from its use. We use the term "depreciation" to specifically describe the amortization of plant assets. We say natural resources are "depleted". When we allocate a portion of an intangible asset as a cost, we say it has been "amortized". In each case there is one common idea: each period, we attempt to allocate the cost of using a capital asset in that period.

Answer to Question Two

When we include costs incurred to get an asset into use with the acquisition cost, we say we are capitalizing these costs. What is the alternative? To report them directly on the income statement as expenses.

Accountants do not have the freedom to choose. The Cost Principle clearly states the acquisition cost of an asset includes all costs needed to get it up and running. Often many costs other than the invoice cost of the asset must be incurred. Accountants tie these other costs with the asset purchase price in determining the acquisition cost. Capitalization is the process of including these costs together. Since we amortize the entire acquisition cost, we may say these other expenditures have been capitalized.

Answer to Question Three

Three estimation problems arise in allocating amortization costs. We must determine how much of the cost of the asset is subject to amortization. This is not simply the acquisition cost. The acquisition cost must be adjusted for any value that is expected to be received upon disposal of the asset, or costs, e.g., dismantling, associated with the disposal. That gives rise to a second forecast; an estimation of its service life - how long the company expects to keep the asset in use. The third problem concerns estimating the cost pattern while the asset is in use.

Since assets may be used in a variety of ways, many different cost patterns exist to reflect specific usage. They fall within the range of immediate write-off to no amortization whatsoever. For example, if an asset's value is completely diminished the very first time it is used its cost pattern must allow for expensing the full acquisition price immediately. At the opposite extreme, if the asset will never decline in value then the cost pattern reflects this and zero amortization is taken. Generally speaking, land is such an asset.

Most assets are not fully used up on day one, nor never used up. Therefore, most cost patterns fall within these two extremes. The most common patterns used in financial accounting are: accelerated, constant and units of activity.

Answer to Question Four

For the first four years of operation the annual depreciation expense is: ($22,000 - $2,000) ÷ 10 years = $2,000 per year.

Therefore, the accumulated depreciation balance will be: 4 years x $2,000 = $8,000.

The amount of depreciation not yet taken equals its carrying value: $22,000 - $8,000 = $14,000.

Therefore, the revised annual depreciation charge beginning in 2014 is: ($14,000 - $1,000) ÷ (6 years – 4 years) = $6,500 per year.

Answer to Question Five

Typically, the cost of using capital assets follows an accelerated, constant or an activity-based pattern.

Accelerated means most of the cost of usage happens quickly. We speed up the expensing of the asset. That is, the value of the asset declines rapidly during the early years of its service life. Thus, the amortization expense will be greatest in the first accounting period and then decline each subsequent period. The declining-balance method is an accelerated approach.

Constant refers to a pattern where the usage cost is the same in each year of the asset's life, assuming there are no revisions to either the service life or salvage value of the asset. The depreciation expense is the same each period. The Straight-line depreciation method follows a constant cost pattern.

When the cost pattern does not either accelerate or remain constant with time, it may be completely dependent on how actively the depreciable asset, e.g., a machine, is used. Once the total output is achieved, the service life of the machine has expired. The productive-output method is an example of activity based depreciation.

Answer to Question Six

You must first determine the annual depreciation expense:

($165,000 - $13,000) ÷ 12 years = $12,667 per year.

Since the asset is disposed of at the beginning of March, four months of depreciation have taken place: November 2013, December 2013, January 2014 and February 2014 and should now be expensed:

Date March 1, 2014	**Debit**	**Credit**
Depreciation Expense	$4,222	
Accumulated Depreciation		$4,222
To record the depreciation for the first 4 months of the business year.		

Computation:
$12,667 x 4 / 12 months = $4,222 for four months.

Now, the gain or loss on disposal must be computed and recorded along with the disposal:

Date March 1, 2014	**Debit**	**Credit**
Cash	$100,000	
Accumulated Depreciation	$62,222*	
Loss on Disposal of Equipment	$ 2,778**	
Equipment		$165,000
To record the disposal of equipment.		

Computations:
**$58,000 + $4,222 = $62,222*
***$165,000 - $62,222 = $102,778 (the carrying value of the equipment on March 1, 2014). Because it was sold at a price less than its carrying value, there is a loss on disposal, namely: $100,000 - $102,778 = - $2,778.*

Practice Problems for Chapter Four

Question One

Today, the Neoplolitian Corporation purchased with cash a new machine to be used in its production process. The invoice price was $120,000. In addition, $15,000 cash was spent for delivery, engineering and set-up costs. Management estimates the machine will be used for five years to produce a total of 63,500 units, after which time it will be sold for $8,000.

As the bookkeeper, you are unsure about which depreciation method is best for this machine. After thinking about it and conducting some research, you have discovered the following:

- If the service life of the machine is 5 years then the machine's value might decline at a constant rate of 1 / 5 or 20% each year.

- The production manager believes the machine will be used as follows:

Year	Estimated Number of Units produced
1	13,500
2	20,000
3	20,000
4	8,000
5	2,000

Calculate the annual depreciation expense, accumulated depreciation, carrying value and any end of life adjustments needed for this machine using the straight-line, declining-balance and productive-output approaches. Complete the tables provided on the next page and, in each case, indicate the name of the method you are using.

Method: ______________________________

Computation:

Start of Year	Acquisition Cost (1)	Accumulated Depreciation (2)	Carrying Value (1) - (2) = (3)	Annual Depreciation Expense (4)
1				
2				
3				
4				
5				
End of Year 5				

Method: ______________________________

Start of Year	Acquisition Cost (1)	Accumulated Depreciation (2)	Carrying Value (1) - (2) = (3)	Depreciation Rate (4)	Annual Depreciation Expense (3) x (4) = (5)
1				20%	
2				20%	
3				20%	
4				20%	
5				20%	
End of Year 5				Adjustment	*

*Computatiom:

Method: ______________________________

Computation:

Start of Year	Acquisition Cost (1)	Accumulated Depreciation (2)	Carrying Value (1) - (2) = (3)	Units Produced (4)	Depreciation Cost per Rate	Annual Depreciation Expense (4) x (5) = (6)
1						
2						
3						
4						
5						
End of Year 5						

Which depreciation method do you think is most appropriate? Why?

____

____

____

____

Question Two

Use the information provided in Question One. For simplicity, assume the management of Neoplolitian Corporation elected to use straight-line depreciation, to capture the cost of using this machine.

After two full years of using the machine, management paid $40,000 cash at the beginning of the third year for major improvements to the machine. These betterments increased both the service life and disposal value. The revised estimates are a total 7-year service life and a $10,000 disposal value.

Finally, after using the machine for seven years, the management of Neoplolitian Corporation disposed of it at the end of the seventh year for $7,500 cash.

Record all the journal entries relating to the acquisition, use and disposal of this machine in the general journal provided below:

Neoplolitian Corporation – General Journal

Date:	Debit	Credit

Computation:

Date:	Debit	Credit

Computation:

Date:	Debit	Credit

Date:	Debit	Credit

Workspace for revised depreciation calculations as a result of the improvement:

Date:	Debit	Credit

*Computation:

Date:	Debit	Credit

Date:	Debit	Credit

Date:	Debit	Credit

Date:	Debit	Credit

Date:	Debit	Credit

Computations:

Solutions to Practice Problems for Chapter Four

Solutions to Question One

***Method:** Straight-line*
Computation:
($120,000 + $15,000 - $8,000) ÷ 5 years = $25,400 per year

Start of Year	Acquisition Cost (1)	Accumulated Depreciation (2)	Carrying Value (1) - (2) = (3)	Annual Depreciation Expense (4)
1	$135,000	$ 0	$135,000	$25,400
2	$135,000	$ 25,400	$109,600	$25,400
3	$135,000	$ 50,800	$ 84,200	$25,400
4	$135,000	$ 76,200	$ 58,800	$25,400
5	$135,000	$101,600	$ 33,400	$25,400
End of Year 5	$135,000	$127,000	$ 8,000	

This method assumes the machine is used equally in each year of its life. If the production schedule is accurate, and most of the production takes place in the first three years, and also if the units are sold as they are produced, then this method may not accurately match the costs with revenues for each accounting period.

Method: Declining-balance

Start of Year	Acquisition Cost (1)	Accumulated Depreciation (2)	Carrying Value (1) - (2) = (3)	Depreciation Rate (4)	Annual Depreciation Expense (3) x (4) = (5)
1	$135,000	$ 0	$135,000	20%	$27,000
2	135,000	$27,000	$108,000	20%	$21,600
3	135,000	$48,600	$ 86,400	20%	$17,280
4	135,000	$65,880	$ 69,120	20%	$13,824
5	135,000	$79,704	$ 55,296	20%	$11,059.20
End of Year 5	135,000	$90,763.20	$ 8,000	Adjustment	$36,236.80*

**Computation:*

The carrying value should equal the disposal cost of $8,000 for this machine at the end of year five. Actually, the unadjusted carrying value is $44,236.80 ($135,000 - $90,763.20) at the end of year 5. We increase the year five depreciation expense by $36,236.80 ($44,236.80 - $8,000) to resolve the problem.

Clearly, if such a large adjustment is needed, the depreciation method did not do a very good job of measuring the true cost pattern. Thus, declining balance does not seem appropriate in this case.

Computation:

Depreciation cost per unit = (\$135,000 - \$8,000) ÷ 63,500
= \$2.00 per unit

Method: Productive-output

Start of Year	Acquisition Cost (1)	Accumulated Depreciation (2)	Carrying Value (1) - (2) = (3)	Units Produced (4)	Depreciation Cost per Rate	Annual Depreciation Expense (4) x (5) = (6)
1	\$135,000	\$ 0	\$135,000	13,500	\$2.00	\$27,000
2	135,000	\$ 27,000	\$108,000	20,000	\$2.00	\$40,000
3	135,000	\$ 67,000	\$ 68,000	20,000	\$2.00	\$40,000
4	135,000	\$107,000	\$ 28,000	8,000	\$2.00	\$16,000
5	135,000	\$123,000	\$ 12,000	2,000	\$2.00	\$ 4,000
End of Year 5	135,000	\$127,000	\$ 8,000	63,500		

At the end of year five the acquisition cost less the accumulated depreciation equals the carrying value; it is the same as the disposal value, which we are assuming is unchanged from our initial estimate. That is: \$135,000 - \$127,000 = \$8,000.

As no adjustments are needed and if the estimate of the total units produced is reasonably accurate, then this method will best match the cost of using the machine to the revenue it produces, in each accounting period.

Solutions to Question Two

Neoplolitian Corporation – General Journal

Date: Acquisition date, Year One	Debit	Credit
Machinery	\$135,000	
Cash		\$135,000
To record the purchase of a machine for \$135,000.		

Computation:

\$120,000 + \$15,000 = \$135,000

Date: End of annual accounting period, Year One	*Debit*	*Credit*
Depreciation Expense	*$25,400*	
Accumulated Depreciation		*$25,400*
To record the depreciation for the machine for the first annual accounting period.		

Computation:

($135,000 - $8,000) ÷ 5 years = $25,400 per year

Date: End of annual accounting period, Year Two	*Debit*	*Credit*
Depreciation Expense	*$25,400*	
Accumulated Depreciation		*$25,400*
To record the depreciation for the machine for the second annual accounting period.		

Date: End of annual accounting period, Year Three	*Debit*	*Credit*
Machinery (improvements)	*$40,000*	
Cash		*$40,000*
To record the improvement to the machine.		

Revised depreciation calculations as a result of the improvement:

After two years the company has already accumulated $50,800 in depreciation ($25,400 x 2). The improvements extended the service life from 5 to 7 years, or by 2 years. Therefore, 5 years of estimated service life remain. Additionally, the disposal value was increased to $10,000.

Only the undepreciated portion of the asset is affected by the improvement. Therefore:

Cost of asset when acquired	*$135,000*
Less: accumulated depreciation	*(50,800)*
Undepreciated balance	*84,200*
Plus: Cost of improvement	*40,000*
Balance to be depreciated	*$124,200*

Date: End of annual accounting period, Year Three	*Debit*	*Credit*
Depreciation Expense	*$22,840**	
Accumulated Depreciation		*$22,840*
To record the depreciation for the machine for the third annual accounting period.		

***Computation:**

($124,200 - $10,000) ÷ 5 years = $22,840, i.e., 7 years – 2 years = 5 years.

Date: End of annual accounting period, Year Four	*Debit*	*Credit*
Depreciation Expense	*$22,840*	
Accumulated Depreciation		*$22,840*
To record the depreciation for the machine for the fourth annual accounting period.		

Date: End of annual accounting period, Year Five	*Debit*	*Credit*
Depreciation Expense	*$22,840*	
Accumulated Depreciation		*$22,840*
To record the depreciation for the machine for the fifth annual accounting period.		

Date: End of annual accounting period, Year Six	*Debit*	*Credit*
Depreciation Expense	*$22,840*	
Accumulated Depreciation		*$22, 840*
To record the depreciation for the machine for the sixth annual accounting period.		

Date: End of annual accounting period, Year Seven	*Debit*	*Credit*
Depreciation Expense	*$22, 840*	
Accumulated Depreciation		*$22,840*
To record the depreciation for the machine for the seventh annual accounting period.		

Date: End of annual accounting period, Year Seven	*Debit*	*Credit*
Cash	*$ 7,500*	
Accumulated Depreciation	*$165,000**	
Loss on Disposal of Machine	*$ 2,500***	
Equipment		*$175,000 ****
To record the disposal of the machine.		

Computations:

**Accumulated depreciation is the sum of the depreciation expense recorded over the entire period of seven years: (2 x $25,400) + (5 x $22,840) = $165,000. In other words, only the estimated disposal value of $10,000 should not have accumulated as depreciation during this period.*

*** The loss on disposal is the difference between the actual cash received from disposal and the estimated disposal value: $7,500 - $10,000 = -$2,500. Another way to look at this loss is: $7,500 + $165,000 - $175,000 = -$2,500.*

****The value in the equipment account is $135,000 + $40,000 = $175,000.*

Notes

Chapter Five - Liabilities and Preferred Equity

The Reason for This Chapter

In this chapter we look at the right-hand side of the balance sheet in greater detail. Chapter Five examines current and long-term liabilities as well as introducing preferred equity.

The liability accounts generally represent the value of money borrowed from others that must be repaid. Sometimes liabilities represent the value of future services or goods that must be delivered where cash has already been received. As with the carrying value of assets, it may be desirable to report both the original amount borrowed along with the going rate of interest. Together they represent a truer picture of the amount that must be repaid. Just like current and capital assets, liabilities can also be classified as either current or long-term.

The equity accounts reflect the position of the owners of the company. Similar to assets and liabilities, we may classify equity into different types. Our previous books considered Common Equity, only. In this chapter we introduce Preferred Equity.

What Do You Already Know?

Pre-Test

Question One

On August 1, 2014, Steamers Corporation receives a note in exchange for the sale of $15,000 worth of merchandise from its customer, Bearings Ltd. The interest-bearing note will be repaid at the end of three months. The principal amount of the note is $15,000 and the annual interest rate is 8%. How much interest will Steamers Corporation earn if it holds the note until it matures? Prepare the necessary journal entries to report this transaction in the space provided below. You may ignore the entry for Cost of Goods Sold:

Steamers Corporation – General Journal

Date	Debit	Credit

Date	Debit	Credit

***Computation:**

Question Two

On November 1, 2014, Newtown Incorporated declared its intention to pay a $0.55 dividend per share to all holders of record at November 30, 2014. The dividend checks will be mailed 31 days after the record date. On November 1, 2014 there are 1,000,000 authorized no par value common shares, and 350,000 shares are outstanding. It is not expected that any additional shares will be issued before December 31, 2014. Record the necessary journal entries.

Newtown Incorporated – General Journal

Date	Debit	Credit

Computation:

Date	Debit	Credit

Question Three

Cantell Corporation has 2,000,000 authorized par-value common shares. The par-value of each share is $1. On June 3, 2014, the company issues 5,000 shares for cash, at a price of $20 each. Record the journal entry for the share issuance in the space provided below:

Cantell Corporation – General Journal

Date	Debit	Credit

Computations:

Answers to Pre-Test

Answer to Question One

Steamers Corporation – General Journal

Date *August 1, 2014*	*Debit*	*Credit*
Notes Receivable	*$15,000*	
Sales Revenue		*$15,000*
To record the sale of merchandise in exchange for a 3-month 8% interest-bearing note from Bearings Ltd.		

Date October 31, 2014	**Debit**	**Credit**
Cash	$15,300	
Notes Receivable		$15,000
Interest Revenue		$300*
To record the collection of a three-month interest-bearing note plus the interest from Bearings Ltd.		

***Computation:**
$15,000 x 8% = $1,200 interest per year.
$1,200 x 3/12 = $300 interest for three months.

Answer to Question Two

Newtown Incorporated – General Journal

Date November 1, 2014	**Debit**	**Credit**
Retained Earnings	$192,500	
Dividends Payable		$192,500
To record a declared dividend of $0.55 per share on 350,000 outstanding common shares.		

Computation:
350,000 x $0.55 = $192,500.

Date December 31, 2014*	**Debit**	**Credit**
Dividends Payable	$192,500	
Cash		$192,500
To record the payment of the $0.55 per share declared dividend.		

**Note: the payment date is 31 days after the November 30, 2014 record date.*

Answer to Question Three

Cantell Corporation – General Journal

Date *June 3, 2014*	**Debit**	**Credit**
Cash	*$100,000**	
Share Capital		*$5,000***
Additional Paid-In Capital		*$95,000****
To record the issuance of 5,000 common shares with par-value of $1 each, sold for $20 each.		

Computations:

**5,000 x $20 = $100,000.*

*** 5,000 x $1 = $5,000.*

****5,000 x ($20 - $1) = $95,000.*

How This Chapter Relates to Other Chapters in This Book

This book is about how accountants classify and carry account values on the balance sheet. While the other financial statements remain important, the emphasis given here relies mainly on those permanent accounts.

In Chapter One we classified and carried current assets. This called for an introduction to the notion of Lower of Cost or Market. In Chapter Two we examined one current asset in greater detail: inventory.

Chapter Four highlighted how we should carry assets classified as longer-term, or capital assets. This chapter demonstrates the classification of liabilities as well as a brief overview of their carrying values. It also introduces a new classification of equity: Preferred Shares.

What Are the Topics in This Chapter?

Past chapters in this series of books examined interest revenue calculations, accounts payable and bank loans along with issuing equity and dividend declarations. In this chapter we revisit each of these topics in greater detail. We also explore related topics not yet seen. This chapter explores the right-hand side of the balance sheet: liabilities and equity.

Topics Covered in Chapter Five	*Level of Importance*
About Liabilities	
Definition	***
Classification	***
Measurement	***
The Cost Principle, again	***
Current Liabilities	
Accounts Payable	***
Short-term Notes Payable	***
Other Current Liabilities	**
Long-term Liabilities	
Long-term Notes Payable	***
Bonds Payable	**
Accounting for Bonds Issued at Par	***
Other Long-term Liabilities	*
Preferred Shares	
Special Characteristics	**
Accounting for Preferred Share Issues	**

About Liabilities

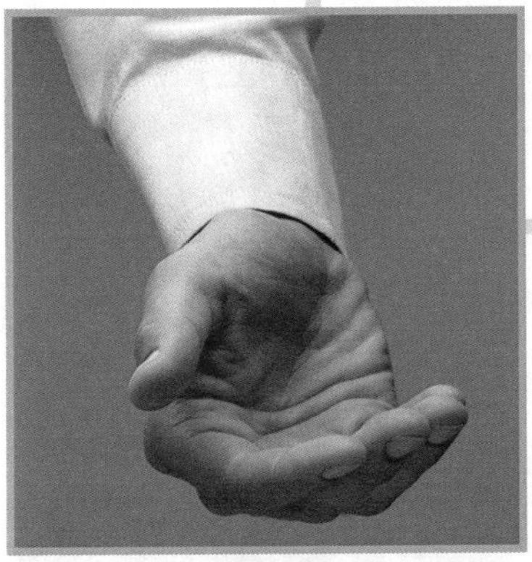

Definition

When you borrow money you create a liability. You, the borrower, are obliged to repay the lender by some date in the future. Thus, a liability is an obligation from the past that requires settlement in future, usually by payment or payments on specific dates. Also known as debt or obligations, liabilities must be repaid. Lenders generally have the right to pursue legal action against borrowers for any debts not repaid in a timely manner.

Size and time of repayment are both important elements to account for when reporting liabilities. In business, very often money borrowed will not be repaid on just one date. Longer-term obligations are usually repaid over several years. Under the accrual system we potentially record these obligations on two dates: when they are due and when they are paid.

Classification

Like assets, we classify liabilities in order of their maturity. A business will normally have both short and long-term obligations, so we list them as such. Current or short-term debt is that which matures within one year or the operating cycle, which ever is longer. Most bank loans or promissory notes and payables fall within this category. We report any liability with a maturity date greater than one year as long-term debt.

Measurement

Every liability consists of two different components: interest and principal. The principal represents the original amount borrowed and thus is the amount due on the maturity date. Interest is like rent that must be paid for using the money until it is repaid. While many different styles of debt exist, usually periodic interest is paid on the amount of money owed. Commonly, two relevant dates occur, the interest dates and the maturity date.

The Cost Principle, Again

Using the cost principal, we record liabilities at the value of resources received on the date the obligation is entered into. This is almost always the principal or amount of money initially borrowed. We also call it the maturity or face value. When this debt is due within a year we often describe it as an interest-bearing note.

At least two exceptions to the cost principle exist: 1) non-interest-bearing notes, and 2) unrealistic interest rate. In the first case the obligation is originally created to include the interest payment with the maturity value. While the interest rate is not specifically mentioned, it is still implied. Interest equals the difference between the amount borrowed and the amount repaid. In the second case we utilize mathematical techniques to account for the difference. Brief coverage is provided in the section dealing with Bonds Payable, later in this chapter.

The name non-interest-bearing is really misleading because all loans, including this type of loan, contain an interest portion. In this case the face value will be different from the amount borrowed. The difference is the interest contained in the note. We use the contra liability account "Discount on Note Payable" to account for it. In this way the balance sheet reflects the proper carrying value of the liability - the difference between the amount borrowed and the interest to be paid.

We examined interest-bearing notes and introduced non-interest-bearing notes in Chapter Five, Volume Two of the first series. Try Learning Exercise One as a review. Attempt Learning Exercise Two as a challenge.

Now You Try It

Learning Exercise One

Win Choo Ltd. signs an interest-bearing note promising to pay Global Incorporated for $33,000 of merchandise purchased on July 1, 2014. The amount must be repaid within six months. The face value of the note equals the merchandise value, and the annual rate of interest is 10%. Win Choo Ltd. repays the note at the end of the six- month period as promised, with interest. Record journal entries for this transaction in the appropriate space provided. Assume Win Choo Ltd. uses the periodic inventory system (and thus a "Purchases" account).

Win Choo Ltd – General Journal

Date	Debit	Credit

Date	Debit	Credit

Computation:

Answers

Answer to Learning Exercise One

Win Choo Ltd – General Journal

Date *July 1, 2014*	**Debit**	**Credit**
Purchases	*$33,000*	
Note Payable		*$33,000*
To record the purchase of merchandise in exchange for a six-month 10% interest-bearing note to Global Incorporated.		

Date *December 31, 2014*	**Debit**	**Credit**
Note Payable	*$33,000*	
Interest Expense	*$1,650**	
Cash		*$34,650***
To record the payment of a six-month interest-bearing note plus the interest to Global Incorporated.		

Computation:

**$33,000 x 10% = $3,300 interest per year.*

$3,300 x 6/12 = $1,650 interest for six months.

***$33,000 + $1,650 = $34,650.*

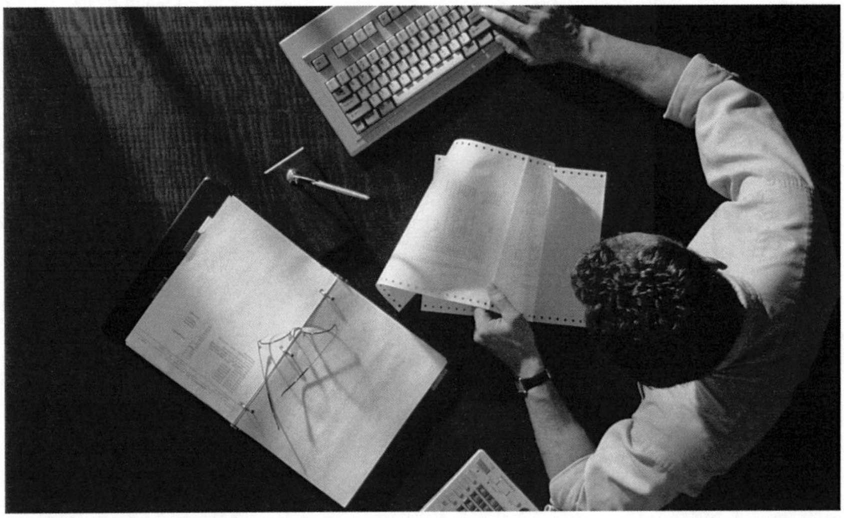

Now You Try It

Learning Exercise Two

Abu Dubai Corporation signs a non-interest-bearing note promising to pay Global Incorporated for $33,000 of merchandise purchased on July 1, 2014. The amount must be repaid within six months. The face value of the note equals $34,650. Abu Dubai Corporation repays the note at the end of the six- month period as promised, with interest. Record the journal entries for this transaction for Abu Dubai Corporation in the appropriate space provided. Assume Abu Dubai uses the periodic inventory system (and thus a "Purchases" account).

Abu Dubai Corporation – General Journal

Date	Debit	Credit

Computation:

Date	Debit	Credit

Answers

Answer to Learning Exercise Two

Abu Dubai Corporation – General Journal

Date *July 1, 2014*	**Debit**	**Credit**
Purchases	$33,000	
Discount on Note Payable	$ 1,650*	
Note Payable (non-interest-bearing)		$34,650
To record the purchase of merchandise in exchange for a six-month non-interest-bearing note to Global Incorporated.		

Computation:

*$34,650 - $33,000 = $1,650 *which is the six-months of interest included in the face value of the non-interest-bearing note as the value of purchases was only* $33,000. *We will not report the interest expense until the interest has been earned by the other party through the passage of time. The balance sheet will reflect the carrying value, or true principal amount of the liability:*

Note Payable	$34,650
Less: Discount on Note Payable	($1,650)
Carrying Value	**$33,000**

Date *December 31, 2014*	*Debit*	*Credit*
Note Payable	*$34,650*	
Interest Expense	*$1,650*	
Discount on Note Payable		*$1,650*
Cash		*$34,650*
To record the payment of a six-month non-interest-bearing note including the interest to Global Incorporated.		

With the passage of time, interest has been earned. We reduced the Discount on Note Payable account balance to zero by crediting the discount account, and recorded Interest Expense by debiting that account.

Current Liabilities

Typically, the order of liabilities on the balance sheet is: Accounts Payable, Short-term Notes Payable and Other Current Liabilities. We examine each, next.

Accounts Payable

Although we have used this account extensively throughout all the volumes in this series, we review it here.

This liability results from purchasing goods or services on account. Most trade credit accounts are due within thirty days of the purchase and no interest is charged. As this trade credit is understood to have a very short life, we record Accounts Payable at face value. We report this account first in the Current Liabilities section of the balance sheet

.

This trade credit can be subject to many different credit terms. Most commonly goods are sold 2/10 net 30 - that is a 2% discount off the invoice amount if the account is paid in full within 10 days of the invoice date. When the business expects to take the discount, it should record the payable at the discounted amount. A full discussion on terms of sale can be found in Chapter Five, Volume Two of the first series. Try Learning Exercise Three.

Now You Try It

Learning Exercise Three

On May 5, 2014, Marbella Incorporated purchases $58,000 worth of merchandise from the Export Trading Company. Terms of sale are 2/10 net 30. Marbella Incorporated always takes the discount and pays its account on the last day of the discount period. Also, Marbella uses the periodic inventory system. Using the space provided below, record the journal entries for this transaction:

Marbella Incorporated – General Journal

Date	Debit	Credit

Computations:

Date	Debit	Credit

Answers

Answer to Learning Exercise Three

Marbella Incorporated – General Journal

Date May 5, 2014	**Debit**	**Credit**
Purchases	$56,840	
Accounts Payable		$56,840
To record merchandise purchased on account.		

Computations:

$58,000 x 2% = $1,160.

$58,000 - $1,160 = $56,840

Date May 15, 2014	**Debit**	**Credit**
Accounts Payable	$56,840	
Cash		$56,840
To record payment of merchandise purchased on account.		

Short-term Notes Payable

A more formal credit arrangement, Notes Payable, may be either short or long-term depending on the stated maturity date. The specific terms of this credit vehicle are formally documented on paper, with each note or loan subject to its own terms. Bank loans can be either a short or long-term note payable. We examined two types of short-term notes, interest-bearing and non-interest-bearing, in the Self-Test and Learning Exercises One and Two.

Other Current Liabilities

Accrued Expenses, Payroll Liabilities and Deferred Revenues tend to follow short-term notes payable on the balance sheet.

Accrued Expenses arise when expenses have been incurred, but not yet paid. Typical examples include Wages Payable and Income Taxes Payable. We record these adjusting entries at the end of each accounting period.

Now You Try It

Learning Exercise Four

On January 31, 2015, the Income Tax Expense for Uhraha Company is calculated to be $21,500. On that date the income tax expense had neither been recorded nor paid. On February 28, 2015 the income tax expense for the month is determined to be $17,890. On March 31, 2015 the Uhraha Company pays $30,000 in income taxes. On that date the income tax expense for the month of March is calculated to be $24,580. Use the space provided to record the journal entries for the first quarter for Uhraha Company. On April 1, 2015, how much income tax does Uhraha Company still owe? Assume that the balance in the Income Taxes Payable account was zero at the beginning of 2015.

Uhraha Company – General Journal

Date	Debit	Credit

Date	Debit	Credit

Date	Debit	Credit

Date	Debit	Credit

Uhraha Company – General Ledger

Income Tax Payable	
	21,500
	17,890
30,000	
	24,580
	33,970

Answers

Answer to Learning Exercise Four

Uhraha Company – General Journal

Date January 31, 2015	**Debit**	**Credit**
Income Tax Expense	$21,500	
Income Tax Payable		$21,500
To record the Income Tax Expense for the month of January 2015, incurred but not yet paid.		

Date February 28, 2015	**Debit**	**Credit**
Income Tax Expense	$17,890	
Income Tax Payable		$17,890
To record the Income Tax Expense for the month of February 2015, incurred but not yet paid.		

Date March 31, 2015	**Debit**	**Credit**
Income Tax Payable	$30,000	
Cash		$30,000
To record the partial payment of Income Tax for the first quarter of 2015.		

Date March 31, 2015	**Debit**	**Credit**
Income Tax Expense	$24,580	
Income Tax Payable		$24,580
To record the Income Tax Expense for the month of March 2015, incurred but not yet paid.		

The ledger reflects the current amount outstanding in each account. On April 1, 2015 the Income Tax Payable T-Account for Uhraha Company would show:

Uhraha Company – General Ledger

Income Tax Payable	
	21,500
	17,890
30,000	
	24,580
	33,970

Thus, on April 1, 2015, Uhraha Company owes $33,970 in income tax payments.

In addition to the salaries or wages an employer must pay, several other liabilities arise in conjunction with the payroll expense. These include withholdings for Federal Income Tax and FICA Tax along with various health and insurance benefit premiums. Chapter Three in *Fundamentals of Accounting: Volume Three* is entitled "Payroll and Taxes". It provides a comprehensive discussion of Payroll liabilities. We invite you to review that chapter.

Deferred Revenues represent revenues that have not yet been earned, but an asset, usually cash, has been received in advance by the seller. For example, a service has not yet been performed, yet the cash for it has been collected. Deferred revenues are a liability because the seller has an *obligation* to perform a service or deliver goods in the future so that the revenue is actually *earned.* Once the goods are delivered or the service takes place we debit Deferred Revenues and credit a revenue account through an adjusting entry. We refer you to Chapter One in *Fundamentals of Accounting: Volume Two* entitled "Adjusting Entries" should you need a review of Accruals or Deferrals. Test your skill. Try Learning Exercise Five.

Now You Try It

Learning Exercise Five

The Singh Corporation receives rent checks from its commercial tenants several times each year. Rent is always paid in advance. On November 1, 2014 Timer Clocks Ltd. gives an $8,000 check to the Singh Corporation to cover its rent for the next four months, (November 2014 through February 2015). The Singh Corporation prepares its financial statements each month. Show the journal entries related to this transaction for Singh Corporation, for the month of November, in the appropriate space provided.

Singh Corporation – General Journal

Date	Debit	Credit

Date	Debit	Credit

Computation:

Answers

Answer to Learning Exercise Five

Singh Corporation – General Journal

Date November 1, 2014	**Debit**	**Credit**
Cash	$8,000	
Rent Revenue Collected in Advance		$8,000
(Deferred Revenue)		
To record rent revenue paid in advance for the next four months by Timer Clocks Ltd.		

Date November 30, 2014	**Debit**	**Credit**
Rent Revenue Collected in Advance	$2,000	
Rent Revenue		$2,000
To record the rent revenue earned for the month of November from Timer Clocks Ltd.		

Computation:
$8,000 ÷ 4 months = $2,000 per month.

At the end of each accounting period, Singh Corporation uses an adjusting entry to reduce the liability account "Rent Revenue Collected in Advance". At the end of four months this deferred revenue account will have a zero balance, as all the rent revenue will have been earned.

Long-term Liabilities

These include all obligations of the business not classified as current liabilities. The business usually negotiates specific terms and dates of repayment for these liabilities as they will not be repaid entirely in the current year. We examine Notes and Bonds Payable, next.

Long-term Notes Payable

This formal document is a promise to pay a stated amount on one or more future dates. Payments may be one lump sum at the end of the loan period, or several installment payments during the loan period. Notes Payable may either be secured or unsecured. When a specific asset is pledged as collateral to the Note Payable, we say the debt is secured. We may also say we have a mortgage. When no specific assets are pledged, the debt is unsecured. That means it is backed by the general ability of the business, not by any one asset.

When you borrow money to purchase a home, your liability is called a mortgage. The debt is secured because your home is used as collateral to support the loan. If you fail to make any of the promised payments, the bank may sell your home and use the proceeds to satisfy the mortgage payments. A corporate mortgage works the same way. Typically, corporate mortgages involve costly items such as buildings or equipment.

Because long-term Notes Payable will be repaid over several accounting periods, accountants use adjusting entries to account for the difference between the time interest is incurred and when it is actually paid. As the long-term debt approaches its maturity date, the part of it owed in the current period must be reported as a current liability. We reflect this on the balance sheet by carrying the maturing portion of the long-term note in the current liabilities section.

Now You Try It

Learning Exercise Six

On January 1, 2014, the Singh Corporation borrows $30,000 at a rate of 10% per year from United Bank with a formal promise to repay the money over the next two years in equal installments. Specifically, on each December 31, Singh Corporation will make principal payments of $15,000. In addition, Singh Corporation will make a cash interest payment once a year.

However, Singh Corporation closes its books every six months - that is, each June and December. Show Singh Corporation's journal entries for this loan, for the first year.

Singh Corporation – General Journal

Date	Debit	Credit

Date	Debit	Credit

***Computation:**

Date	Debit	Credit

***Computation:**

How is the unpaid portion of the note reported on the balance sheet dated December 31, 2014?

___

___

___

___

Answers

Answer to Learning Exercise Six

Singh Corporation – General Journal

Date January 1, 2014	**Debit**	**Credit**
Cash	$30,000	
Note Payable - long-term		$30,000
To record the receipt of a 2 year long-term note payable from United Bank at 10%, with equal installments.		

Date June 30, 2014	**Debit**	**Credit**
Interest Expense	$1,500*	
Interest Payable		$1,500
To record the interest incurred on the United Bank loan but not yet paid.		

***Computation:**

$30,000 x 10% = $3,000 per year.
$3,000 ÷ 2 = $1,500 per six months.

Date December 31, 2014	**Debit**	**Credit**
Interest Expense	$1,500	
Interest Payable	$1,500	
Note Payable	$15,000	
Cash		$18,000*
To record the payment of interest and principal on the United Bank loan.		

***Computation:**

$15,000 principal + $3,000 interest.

On December 31, 2014 the $15,000 maturing portion of the Note Payable should be reclassified from long-term liabilities to the current liabilities section of the balance sheet to reflect that it will be paid in the upcoming year.

Bonds Payable

A bond is a long-term promissory note used by large corporations and many governments. Bonds have marketability when they trade in an organized exchange. The bond market is similar to the stock market except long-term liabilities are traded instead of corporate equity.

While many different kinds of bonds exist, we examine only the most common features here. Bonds may be either secured or unsecured. Like Notes Payable, most bonds have the same three basic components: the face or par value, the stated interest or coupon rate and term to maturity. Unlike Notes Payable, bonds also have a market rate of interest.

The life of this debt is very long-term - twenty to forty years is quite common. Since the bond's life spans such a long period of time, it is likely economic conditions will change during that time. This means the bond's stated rate of interest will no longer reflect current market or economic conditions. Instead of changing the stated rate, the market price of a bond changes to reflect the difference between the stated interest rate and the market interest rate. If the two are different at the time of issue, we account for the difference using a process known as Effective Interest Amortization.

This topic is far beyond the scope of this book for the following reason. In order to calculate the change in a bond's price due to interest rate changes, sophisticated mathematical formulae must be applied. This concept, known as the time value of money requires either laborious calculations, the use of a scientific calculator or prepared financial tables. Without this effort we cannot capture the change in price.

When the stated rate and market rates of interest are the same, the bond's price is generally equal to its par value. We examine accounting for bonds at par, next.

Accounting for Bonds Issued at Par

When a bond is created or issued, the rate of interest that will be paid over its life is known as the stated rate of interest, or coupon rate. We calculate the periodic cash interest payments by simply multiplying the bond's stated rate by its par value. In North America the interest on most bonds is paid every six months. Default on these payments carries serious financial consequences for the corporation and only happens when the company is in serious trouble.

Normally, if the stated rate of interest is the same as the market rate of interest at the time the bonds are issued, the cash received by the issuing corporation will equal the face value of the bonds. Of course there are additional costs associated with issuing bonds such as legal fees and brokerage fees. . Accounting for bonds in this case is very straightforward. The carrying value on the balance sheet will equal the par value of the bonds. We use the same process to account for the interest payments as with an interest-bearing note.

When there is a difference between the stated rate of interest and the market rate of interest at the time of issuance, the bonds will not be issued at par. Instead there will either be a discount or a premium. This difference is amortized using a method such as effective interest amortization.

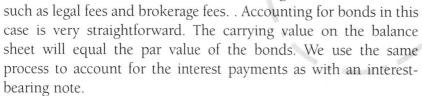

Now You Try It

Learning Exercise Seven

On January 1, 2014, Maakko Corporation issued $20 million worth of 20 year bonds at a stated rate of 12%. The company will make semi-annual coupon interest payments each June 30 and December 31. Assuming the market rate of interest also remains at 12%, record the journal entries for the first year of the bond in the space provided.

Maakko Corporation – General Journal

Date	Debit	Credit

Date	Debit	Credit

Computation:

Date	Debit	Credit

Answers

Answer to Learning Exercise Seven

Maakko Corporation – General Journal

Date *January 1, 2014*	***Debit***	***Credit***
Cash	*20,000,000*	
Bonds Payable		*20,000,000*
To record the issue of $20 million 20 year bonds with a stated rate of 12%.		

Date June 30, 2014	Debit	Credit
Bond Interest Expense	1,200,000	
Cash		1,200,000
To record the cash interest payment for the first six months of 2014.		

Computation:

\$20,000,000 x 12% = \$2,400,000 per year.

\$2,400,000 ÷ 2 = \$1,200,000 every six months.

Date December 31, 2014	Debit	Credit
Bond Interest Expense	1,200,000	
Cash		1,200,000
To record the cash interest payment for the second six months of 2014.		

Other Long-term Liabilities

Two other long-term liability accounts are often seen on the balance sheet of corporations. These are Deferred Income Tax and Contingent Liabilities.

The Deferred Income Tax account reports the cumulative difference between the reported income tax expense on the income statement and the actual amount of tax the corporation pays to the government. Should a business significantly change its investment strategy, the deferred income tax liability will likely decline. It is important to note this account has nothing to do with the income tax payable account.

Contingent Liabilities represent a potential liability amount resulting from an event that has already occurred. Contingent liabilities might not ever become real liabilities; however the likelihood is they may. A common example of a contingent liability is the potential obligation associated with possible damages resulting from ongoing or pending lawsuits. For some companies contingent liabilities can have a significant impact on future operations.

Preferred Shares

When a business incorporates it must authorize some common shares as evidence of ownership. Corporations may have more than one classification of equity. Many companies use preferred shares in addition to common shares. However, corporations must always issue common shares.

Preferred shares are legally equity but with characteristics different from common equity. Some of these differences are favorable, some unfavorable. We examine each, next.

Special Characteristics

Preferred equity differs from common equity in four main ways. They are with respect to: dividends, conversion, claim on assets and voting.

Preferred dividend payments are usually a pre-determined, fixed amount. They may be stated as a percentage of the preferred share's par value, should the preferred share be issued with a par value. Preferred dividends are usually cumulative. This means if the preferred dividend payment is skipped, it will be accumulated into the future. Until the arrearage, or owed payment is made, common shareholders will not be able to receive any dividend payments. From the perspective of common shareholders, the cumulative feature of the preferred dividend payment forms a kind of liability.

Furthermore, the amount of common dividend payment is determined by management and submitted for approval at the quarterly meeting of the board of directors. It is not a pre-determined fixed amount nor is it ever paid in arrears.

Often Preferred shares offer conversion privileges. This right allows preferred shareholders the ability to convert their preferred shares into a fixed number of common shares. Conversion usually takes place if the business is performing well.

Preferred shares may contain a provision with regards to the dissolution of the business. Should the operations be terminated, preferred shareholders may have the right to claim the assets of the business before common shareholders receive anything. Of course this would be limited to a pre-determined value, and only after all liabilities of the business have been satisfied.

Finally, an unfavorable difference between preferred and common shareholders is the right to vote. While the common shareholder has this right, the preferred shareholder generally does not.

While each of these differences helps to account for the market price of a preferred share, we will not explore this topic any further. Instead we examine how to account for preferred share issues, next.

Accounting for Preferred Share Issues

Recording and reporting preferred share issues is much the same as common shares. However, we use a separate equity account, Preferred Stock, to show the relevant activity. A comprehensive review of accounting for corporate equity can be found in Accounting For Corporations: Volume One. Try Learning Exercise Eight.

Now You Try It

Learning Exercise Eight

The Goldstein Corporation issued 15,000 shares of no-par preferred stock at $30 each for cash on January 1, 2014. The quarterly dividend payment was fixed at $0.90 per share.

Assuming all transactions are for cash, record the journal entries for the first six months of 2014 for Goldstein Corporation in the space provided.

Goldstein Corporation – General Journal

Date	Debit	Credit

Computation:

Date	Debit	Credit

Computation:

Date	Debit	Credit

Answers

Answer to Learning Exercise Eight

Goldstein Corporation – General Journal

Date January 1, 2014	**Debit**	**Credit**
Cash	450,000	
Preferred Stock		450,000
To record the issuance of 15,000 no-par preferred shares at $30 per share.		

Computation:
15,000 x $30 = $450,000.

Date March 31, 2014	**Debit**	**Credit**
Retained Earnings	13,500	
Cash		13,500
To record the quarterly cash dividend payment for the preferred shares at $0.90 per share.		

Computation:
15,000 x $0.90 = $13,500.

Date June 30, 2014	**Debit**	**Credit**
Retained Earnings	13,500	
Cash		13,500
To record the quarterly cash dividend payment for the preferred shares at $0.90 per share.		

Remember, dividends reduce retained earnings. Of course, a cash dividend can only be declared if there is sufficient cash on hand to pay the dividend and still be able to pay other liabilities. Note also that in the first six months of 2014 there are two quarters, namely those ending on March 31 and June 30, respectively.

What You Have Learned in This Chapter

This chapter looked at the right side of the balance sheet in greater detail. Its focus was on the liabilities section. It showed how to classify these obligations into their current and long-term components. In addition, it introduces a few new liability accounts. While many of the topics were touched upon in previous volumes, this chapter increased the level of detail.

This chapter also introduced a new classification of equity - Preferred Stock. While not explored in great detail, the general characteristics of preferred shares were covered.

Reviewing the section "Important Terms in this Chapter" provides a great summary. It serves to test your understanding. If you can define all these terms, you most likely have a good grasp of the topics covered. You will further test this knowledge by completing the Self-Test and Practice Problems. Good Luck.

Important Terms in This Chapter

Accounts Payable: this current liability results from purchasing goods or services on account. While this trade credit can be subject to many different terms, it is widely understood these accounts are due within a matter of days or months, not years.

Accrued Expenses: arise when expenses have been incurred, but not yet paid. We record these adjusting entries at the end of each accounting period.

Bond: a long-term promissory note issued by a corporation or government. Often trades in an organized exchange called the Bond Market.

Collateral: using or pledging an asset to back a loan. The lender may sell the asset if the borrower defaults on any of the loan or interest payments.

Coupon Interest: the cash interest payment determined by multiplying the coupon rate by the face value of a bond.

Coupon Rate: the stated rate of interest on a bond used to determine the cash interest payment.

Current Liability: an obligation maturing within one year or the operating cycle, whichever is longer.

Deferred Revenue: a liability representing an unearned revenue for which the cash (or some other asset) has been received in advance.

Discount on Note Payable: a contra liability account used to account for the difference between the face value and amount borrowed on a noninterest-bearing note. This difference is actually the interest that must still be earned by the lender through the passage of time.

Face Value: usually the same as the principal, or amount owed. It represents the amount that must be repaid on the maturity date.

Interest-bearing Note: a note where the principal amount does not include the interest.

Liability: an obligation from the past that requires settlement in future, usually by payment or payments on specific dates. Also called debt or obligation.

Maturity: the date the obligation becomes due.

Maturity Value: see Face Value.

Mortgage: long-term debt that is backed by a specific asset. If the borrower fails to make any of the promised payments the lender may sell the asset and use its proceeds as payment.

Non-interest-bearing Note: a note where the principal amount includes the interest associated with the note.

Notes Payable: unlike accounts payable this is a more formal credit arrangement and includes specific repayment terms. Can be either short or long-term, interest-bearing or non-interest-bearing.

Par Value: see Face Value.

Preferred Shares: a separate class of equity that may be used by corporations to raise capital. Its features are similar to debt, yet it is legally equity.

Secured Debt: see Mortgage.

Unsecured Debt: is backed by the general ability of the business, not by any one asset.

Should You Move on to the Next Chapter?

It's time to see if you are comfortable with your new knowledge. Complete the Self-Test and Practice Problems to determine whether or not you are ready to move on to the final chapter.

Self-Test for Chapter Five

Question One

Why is deferred revenue a liability? Explain.

Question Two

What is a non-interest-bearing note? Explain.

Question Three

The annual accounting period for Sharni Corporation ends each December 31. During 2014, it completed the following transactions:

1. Wages paid and recorded during 2014 were $200,000, yet at the end of December there was one week of wages earned but not yet paid or recorded in the amount of $3,850. These wages will be paid in January 2015.

2. On December 15, 2014, the company collected rent revenue of $2,500 on office space it rents to another company. The rent collected was for 30 days from December 15, 2014 to January 15, 2015. The full $2,500 was recorded and credited to Rent Revenue on December 15, 2014.

Give the adjusting entry required on December 31, 2014 for each of these transactions in the space provided below:

Sharni Corporation – General Journal

Date	Debit	Credit

Date	Debit	Credit

Computation:

Question Four

On June 30, 2014, Siimply Corporation issued $40 million worth of 25 year bonds at a stated interest rate of 10% per year. The company will make quarterly coupon interest payments at the end of each March, June, September and December. Assuming the market rate of interest at the time of issuance was also 10%, record the journal entries for 2014 in the space provided below.

Siimply Corporation – General Journal

Date June 30, 2014	Debit	Credit

Date	Debit	Credit

Computation:

Date	Debit	Credit

Question Five

The bookkeeper for General Ties Ltd. has asked for your assistance. She has provided you with several account names and balances and requires you to prepare the liabilities section of the General Ties balance sheet, in proper form, dated December 31, 2014. Use the space provided.

Account Name	Account balance on December 31, 2014
Prepaid Rent	$ 3,500
Rent Revenue Collected in Advance	$ 4,600
Income Tax Expense	$ 8,500
Income Tax Payable	$ 12,500
Accounts Payable	$ 22,500
Accounts Receivable	$ 12,700
Wages Expense	$ 8,250
Wages Payable	$ 12,400
Bonds Payable	$100,000
Interest Expense	$ 14,800
Interest Payable	$ 10,000
Note Payable (due in 6 months)	$ 25,000
Preferred Shares	$ 50,000
Common Shares	$200,000
Retained Earnings	$330,000
Note Payable (due in 5 years)	$ 55,000

General Ties Ltd.
Partial Balance Sheet
As at December 31, 2014

Current Liabilities	
Total Current Liabilities	
Long-term Liabilities	
Total Long-term Liabilities	
Total Liabilities	

Answers to Self-Test for Chapter Five

Answer to Question One

A deferred revenue represents the value of a good or service that is owed. It is a revenue that has been paid for but not yet earned. Therefore, since the business is obliged to perform some action in the future, we report the value of this good or service owed as a liability.

Answer to Question Two

The term "non-interest-bearing note" is deceiving because it implies that such a note carries no interest. This is false. Loans pay some kind of interest. The interest rate in this type of note is not explicitly stated, however it may be computed. The interest payment is included in the face value of the note. Thus, interest is determined as the difference between the face value of the note and the amount of money received at the inception of the loan.

Answer to Question Three

Sharni Corporation – General Journal

Date *December 31, 2014*	**Debit**	**Credit**
Wage Expense	*3,850*	
Wages Payable		*3,850*
To record the wage expense incurred but not yet paid.		

Date *December 31, 2014*	**Debit**	**Credit**
Rent Revenue	*1,250*	
Rent Revenue Collected in Advance		*1,250*
To adjust for rent revenue not yet earned.		

Computation:

$2,500 x 1/2 = $1,250. As the rent was for 30 days, one-half is unearned on December 31, 2014.

Answer to Question Four

Siimply Corporation – General Journal

Date *June 30, 2014*	**Debit**	**Credit**
Cash	*40,000,000*	
Bonds Payable		*40,000,000*
To record the issue of $40 million 25 year bonds with a stated interest rate of 10%.		

Date *September 30, 2014*	**Debit**	**Credit**
Bond Interest Expense	*1,000,000*	
Cash		*1,000,000*
To record the cash interest payment for the first three months of the bond issue in 2014.		

Computation:

$40,000,000 x 10% = $4,000,000 per year.

$4,000,000 ÷ 4 = $1,000,000 every three months.

Date December 31, 2014	**Debit**	**Credit**
Bond Interest Expense	1,000,000	
Cash		1,000,000
To record the cash interest payment for the last three months of the bond issue in 2014.		

Note, in 2014 there are only two interest payments since the bonds were issued at the end of June. Thus, the first three- month period ends in September. Remember, that interest must be incurred by the borrower and earned by the lender, before it is recorded.

Question Five

General Ties Ltd.
Partial Balance Sheet
As at December 31, 2014

Current Liabilities	
Accounts Payable	$ 22,500
Income Tax Payable	$ 12,500
Rent Revenue Collected in Advance	$ 4,600
Wages Payable	$ 12,400
Interest Payable	$ 10,000
Note Payable (due in 6 months)	$ 25,000
Total Current Liabilities	$ 87,000
Long-term Liabilities	
Notes Payable (due in 5 years)	$ 55,000
Bonds Payable	$ 100,000
Total Long-term Liabilities	$ 155,000
Total Liabilities	**$ 242,000**

Practice Problems for Chapter Five

Question One

On October 1, 2014 Nyx Corporation borrowed $55,000 cash from the United Bank. The corporation signed an interest-bearing note with a face value of $55,000. The note was due in nine months and carried an interest rate of 9% per year, payable at maturity. The year-end for Nyx Corporation is December 31. Using the space provided, prepare the journal entries for Nyx Corporation to account for this transaction.

Nyx Corporation – General Journal

Date	Debit	Credit

Date	Debit	Credit

Computation:

Date	Debit	Credit

Computation:

Question Two

The records of the Wang Corporation reflect the following balances in the shareholders' equity accounts at December 31, 2014:

Account Name	Account balance
Common shares, no-par, 152,000 shares outstanding	$232,000
Preferred shares, no-par, 8,000, $3.00 annual cumulative dividend	$ 95,000
Retained Earnings	$100,000

No dividends have yet been declared or paid in 2014. If the board of directors is willing to declare all the retained earnings as dividends, what is the maximum dividend payment, per common share for this year? Assume there are no dividends in arrears from previous years on the preferred shares. Show the journal entries in the space provided below:

Wang Corporation – General Journal

Date	Debit	Credit

Computation:

Date	Debit	Credit

Computation:

Question Three

On April 1, 2014, the Straungh Corporation borrows $180,000 at a rate of 6% per year from the Universal Bank with a formal promise to repay the money over the next three years in equal installments. In addition to the annual repayment, Straungh Corporation will make a cash interest payment each March 31, on the amount owing. However, Straungh Corporation closes its books every December 31. Record all the journal entries needed for this loan in the space provided.

Straungh Corporation – General Journal

Date	Debit	Credit

Date	Debit	Credit

***Computation:**

Date	Debit	Credit

***Computation:**

Date	Debit	Credit

*Computation:

Date	Debit	Credit

*Computation:

Date	Debit	Credit

*Computation:

Date	Debit	Credit

*Computation:

Solutions to Practice Problems for Chapter Five

Solutions to Question One

Nyx Corporation – General Journal

Date *October 1, 2014*	**Debit**	**Credit**
Cash	*$55,000*	
Note Payable		*$55,000*
To record the receipt of a 9% nine-month interest-bearing note.		

Date *December 31, 2014*	**Debit**	**Credit**
Interest Expense	*$1,237.50*	
Interest Payable		*$1,237.50*
To record the interest expense incurred on the note payable.		

Computation:

$55,000 x 9% = $4,950 interest for one year.

$4,950 x 3/12 = $1,237.50 interest for three months.

Date *June 30, 2015*	**Debit**	**Credit**
Note Payable	*$55,000*	
Interest Expense	*$2,475**	
Interest Payable	*$1,237.50*	
Cash		*58,712.50***
To record the payment of the note payable, including interest.		

Computation:

**$4,950 x 6/12 = $2,475 interest for six months.*

*** $55,000 + $2,475 + $1,237.50 = $58,712.50.*

Solutions to Question Two

Wang Corporation – General Journal

Date *December 31, 2014*	**Debit**	**Credit**
Retained Earnings	*$24,000*	
Preferred Share Dividend Payable		*$24,000*
To record the declaration of a $3.00 dividend per preferred share .		

Computation:

8,000 x $3.00 = $24,000.

Date *December 31, 2014*	**Debit**	**Credit**
Retained Earnings	*$76,000*	
Dividends Payable		*$76,000*
To record the declaration of a $0.50 dividend per common share .		

Computation:

$100,000 - $24,000 = $76,000.

$76,000 ÷ 152,000 shares = $0.50 per share.

Although it would generally not be a good idea to "payout" all the retained earnings as dividends, the company would be able to declare a $0.50 dividend per common share. Note that the preferred dividends must be paid first, that is before any dividends are paid to the common shareholders.

Solutions to Question Three

Straungh Corporation – General Journal

Date April 1, 2014	**Debit**	**Credit**
Cash	$180,000	
Note Payable - long-term		$180,000
To record the receipt of a 3 year long-term note payable from Universal Bank at 6%, with equal annual installments.		

Date December 31, 2014	**Debit**	**Credit**
Interest Expense	$8,100*	
Interest Payable		$8,100
To record the interest incurred on the Universal Bank loan but not yet paid.		

Computation:

$180,000 x 6% = $10,800 per year.

$10,800 x 9/12 = $8,100 for nine months.

Date March 31, 2015	**Debit**	**Credit**
Interest Expense	$2,700*	
Interest Payable	$8,100	
Note Payable	$60,000**	
Cash		$70,800***
To record annual payment of interest and principal on the Universal Bank loan.		

Computation:

$180,000 x 6% = $10,800 interest per year.

*$10,800 x 3/12 months = $2,700 for three months.

**$180,000 ÷ 3 = $60,000 per year installment payment.

***$60,000 + $2,700 + $8,100 = $70,800.

Note, only $120,000 is now owing on the loan ($180,000 - $60,000).

Date December 31, 2015	**Debit**	**Credit**
Interest Expense	$5,400*	
Interest Payable		$5,400
To record the interest incurred on the Universal Bank loan but not yet paid.		

Computation:

$120,000 x 6% = $7,200 per year.

$7,200 x 9/12 = $5,400 for nine months.

Date March 31, 2016	**Debit**	**Credit**
Interest Expense	$1,800*	
Interest Payable	$5,400	
Note Payable	$60,000**	
Cash		$67,200***
To record annual payment of interest and principal on the Universal Bank loan.		

Computation:

$120,000 x 6% = $7,200 interest per year.

**$7,200 x 3/12 months = $1,800 for three months.*

***$180,000 ÷ 3 = $60,000 per year installment payment.*

****$60,000 + $1,800 + $5,400 = $67,200.*

Note, only $60,000 is now owing on the loan ($120,000 - $60,000).

Date December 31, 2016	**Debit**	**Credit**
Interest Expense	$2,700*	
Interest Payable		$2,700
To record the interest incurred on the Universal Bank loan but not yet paid.		

Computation:

$60,000 x 6% = $3,600 per year.

$3,600 x 9/12 = $2,700 for nine months.

Date March 31, 2017	Debit	Credit
Interest Expense	$900*	
Interest Payable	$2,700	
Note Payable	$60,000**	
Cash		$63,600***
To record the final payment of interest and principal on the Universal Bank loan.		

Computation:

$60,000 x 6% = $3,600 interest per year.

**$3,600 x 3/12 months = $900 for three months.*

***$180,000 ÷ 3 = $60,000 per year installment payment.*

****$60,000 + $900 + $2,700 = $63,600.*

And the loan is fully repaid with interest.

Notes

Notes

Chapter Six - Practicing with Financial Statements

The Reason for This Chapter

Can you prepare the financial statements using the knowledge gained in this book? This chapter gives you the opportunity to arrange the balance sheet in good order by showing the proper classification of accounts and carrying values, where appropriate. To do so, you must rely on the accounting knowledge gained in *Fundamentals of Accounting: Volumes One, Two, and Three,* and *Accounting For Corporations: Volumes One and Two.*

This Chapter consists of two separate case studies, each involving a different three-month period (quarter) for a given company. The company operates a business, but it needs help with its books. As an accountant, you will provide this aid.

In each case we will provide you with transactions, dates, and a brief summary of the company. And we will help you. To guide you through the accounting process we have provided blank forms for each case. All you must do is complete the forms provided!

What Do You Already Know?

In this section of the chapter we ask you to complete a pre-test. It will get you thinking about what you already know about accounting. It will also serve as a quick review of the contents of *Accounting For Corporations: Volume Two.*

If you have difficulties with the pre-test, you should go back and review the previous chapters. After completing the pre-test, check your answers against the ones provided. If they are correct, then attempt the cases in this chapter.

Pre-Test

Question One

On November 1, 2014 Wanton Ltd. purchased some equipment for $340,000. The freight costs were $2,300. In addition, Wanton incurred the following expenditures related to the equipment:

Item	Cost
Major repair before use	$ 2,500
Rewiring of new machine	$ 800
Test – Run	$ 1,200
Minor repair during first year	$ 2,300
Testing before use; labor	$ 780
Relocation of other equipment to accommodate this one	$ 1,700
Installation	$ 700
Operating costs after start-up	$12,900
Miscellaneous costs during first year	$ 8,900
Testing before use; materials	$ 490

Using the information provided above, answer the following 2 questions:

1. What is the carrying value of this machine on November 1, 2014? Describe how to account for any excluded items.

2. If the company depreciates the equipment using 25% declining balance, what is the carrying cost on December 31, 2014, the company's year-end?

Question Two

Buyer Corporation signs a non-interest-bearing note promising to pay Seller Incorporated for $153,000 of merchandise purchased on September 15, 2014. The amount must be repaid within four months. The face value of the note equals $158,100. Buyer Corporation repays the note at the end of the four month period as promised. Record the journal entries for this transaction for Buyer Corporation in the appropriate space provided. Assume that Buyer uses the periodic inventory system (and thus a "Purchases" account) and that June 30 is the fiscal year-end date.

Buyer Corporation – General Journal

Date	Debit	Credit

Computation:

Date	Debit	Credit

Answers to the Pre-Test

Answer to Question One

1. *The carrying cost of the equipment on November 1, 2014 equals $350,470 - the sum of all expenditures needed to get the equipment into running order. These include:*

Item	*Cost $*
Equipment, invoice cost	*340,00*
Freight Costs	*2,300*
Major repair	*2,500*
Rewiring	*800*
Test – Run	*1,200*
Testing before use; labor	*780*
Relocation of other equipment to accommodate this one	*1,700*
Installation	*700*
Testing before use; materials	*490*
TOTAL	*350,470*

All the other items will be expensed to the income statement.

2. *Using 25% declining balance, the first year's depreciation equals:*

   $350,470 x 25% = $87,618 for one year.
   $87,618 x 2/12 = $14,603 for the two months of this year.

   And the carrying value on December 31, 2014 will be:

Equipment	*$350,470*
Less: Accumulated Depreciation	*(14,603)*
Carrying Value	*$335,867*

Answer to Question Two

Buyer Corporation – General Journal

Date *September 15, 2014*	***Debit***	***Credit***
Purchases	*$153,000*	
Discount on Note Payable	*$ 5,100**	
Note Payable (non-interest-bearing)		*$158,100*
To record the purchase of merchandise in exchange for a four-month non-interest-bearing note to Seller Incorporated.		

Computation:
**$158,100 - $153,000 = $5,100 which is the four-months of interest included in the face value of the non-interest-bearing note as the value of purchases was only $153,000.*

Date *January 15, 2015*	***Debit***	***Credit***
Note Payable	*$158,100*	
Interest Expense	*$5,100**	
Discount on Note Payable		*$5,100**
Cash		*$158,100*
To record the payment of a four-month non-interest-bearing note including the interest to Seller Incorporated.		

**$158,100 - $153,000 = $5,100 interest expense incurred. The Discount on Note Payable along with the Note Payable accounts are both reduced to a zero balance.*

How This Chapter Relates to Other Chapters in This Book

This book examines carrying values. Chapters One and Two offered instruction on how to carry current assets. Chapter Four showed the proper way to report capital assets on the balance sheet. Chapter Five covered liabilities; both current and long-term. In addition, it provided an introduction to accounting for preferred share equity. This final chapter permits a review of those chapters along with earlier ones by providing two case studies. These comprehensive cases enable you to demonstrate the accounting skills gained throughout the volumes in this series.

Topics Covered in Chapter Six

Case One
Maarten's Animal Hospital Incorporated- Third Quarter 2014

Case Two
Maarten's Animal Hospital Incorporated - Fourth Quarter 2014

Case One

Maarten's Animal Hospital Incorporated - Third Quarter 2014

Foxy Maarten graduated with her veterinarian license in 2006. After opening her first practice as a sole proprietor in 2007, she incorporated the business in 2010 to accommodate its growth. This was on the advice of her sister, Bunny Maarten, a successful entrepreneur and shareholder in the business.

Foxy Maarten has always enjoyed a stellar reputation. It has enhanced the business' success. For example, Foxy was invited to participate in a local university's cooperative program. It allows students to earn university credits and money while working for Maarten's Animal Hospital. This program means the hospital gets a lot of talented and affordable, although unskilled, help. In addition, the cheaper labor allows Foxy to provide medical assistance to homeless pets.

Foxy has several licensed veterinarians on staff. With her business acumen she actually spends more time administering the business than actually practicing medicine. Not yet content with the size of the business, Foxy has eagerly re-invested profits to help it become a state-of -the-art medical facility for animals.

Expensive equipment has been purchased over the years. With the help of her sister, the business expansion was aided through negotiation of an attractive debt issue. This enabled Maarten's Animal Hospital to purchase a property to house the business. On June 30th of this year, the deal was closed and the property purchased for $490,000.

Recently, Foxy Maarten has felt concerned about how Jay Byrd handled several transactions. As Mr. Byrd left on vacation without completing the third quarter financial statements, Foxy requested Bunny take charge and suggested she make any changes deemed appropriate. Bunny has hired you to prepare the books for her final approval. She has provided you with the second quarter trial balance, transactions for the third quarter along with additional information.

Maarten's Animal Hospital Incorporated
Post-Closing Trial Balance
June 30, 2014

Account	Debit $	Credit $
Cash	25,500	
Temporary Investments	250,300	
Accounts Receivable	4,800	
Medical Supplies Inventory	226,000	
Prepaid Insurance	30,000	
Equipment	590,000	
Real Estate	490,000	
Accumulated Depreciation (Equipment)		162,000
Note Payable		135,000
Accounts Payable		89,200
Salaries Payable		150,000
Wages Payable		38,000
Income Taxes Payable		32,500
Common Share Capital		300,000
Retained Earnings		709,900
TOTAL	1,616,600	1,616,600

Transactions during the third quarter and additional information are as follows: (note some transactions may require more than one journal entry)

1. Purchased $50,000 worth of medical supplies during the quarter, all on account.
2. Sales for the quarter were $550,000 of which $361,000 were on account.
3. The salaries expense is $150,000 each quarter. The wage expense for the third quarter is $42,000. Total cash paid to employees during the quarter is $320,000. Wages are always paid in full before salaries.
4. Various credit customers pay a total of $3,800 on their accounts during the quarter.
5. Maarten's Animal Hospital pays $90,500 to its suppliers for accounts payable.
6. Bunny Maarten feels the Real Estate account should be closed and the balance split between the property's values: land $70,000, building - the remainder.
7. Miscellaneous expenses in the amount of $27,300 are paid in cash. This includes $5,400 of repairs and maintenance to the equipment and the real estate commissions of $15,000 from the purchase of the building.
8. During the quarter the temporary investments were sold for $260,000 cash.

Information relating to adjusting and other entries required at the end of the quarter is as follows:

9. The premium on a one-year insurance policy for the year July 1, 2014 to June 30, 2015 had been paid in full on June 30, 2014.
10. The equipment is depreciated over a 15-year life on a straight-line basis. The estimated salvage value of the equipment is $50,000.
11. The building should be depreciated using the declining balance method at a 5% rate.

12. A physical count at the end of September showed there was $67,000 in medical supplies on hand.

13. On January 1, 2014 a five-year Note Payable with annual interest calculated at 8%, and principal repayment installments of $30,000 per year, was issued. Maarten's Animal Hospital makes a cash installment payment to the bank at the end of each quarter for principal repayment (equal amounts each quarter), and a cash interest payment every six months (at the end of the second and fourth quarters).

14. At the beginning of this quarter Bunny Maarten purchased 1,000 no par value preferred shares for $90 each with a quarterly fixed cumulative dividend of $3.00 per share. At that time the accountant, Jay Byrd placed the cash proceeds into the Common Share Capital account. By the end of this quarter the dividend had not yet been paid, although it had been declared.

15. On the last day of each quarter the company makes a cash income tax payment of $30,000 regardless of the actual income tax expense. Maarten's Animal Hospital is subject to an Income Tax rate of 30%.

Today is September 30, 2014. In order to close the books for the third quarter of 2014 you are required to do the following:

a. Prepare the journal entries to record the transactions for this quarter. The transactions have been accumulated so instead of recording the date, use the transaction number provided.

b. Set up T-accounts and enter the opening balances in the accounts from June 30, 2014. Post the entries from part a) to the T-accounts, creating new ones as needed. Use the transaction numbers as a reference.

c. Prepare an unadjusted Trial Balance as of September 30, 2014.

d. Prepare the adjusting and other entries required at the end of September. Post them to their T-accounts.

e. Prepare an adjusted Trial Balance as of September 30, 2014.

f. Prepare the financial statements for the month of September.

g. Prepare and post the Closing Entries.

h. Prepare a Post-Closing Trial Balance.

i. Answer a question pertaining to financial statement preparation. (The question can be found after part (h) in the pages that follow.)

We have provided space to complete this work. Using these forms will help guide you through all the steps. If you have any space leftover then you have probably made an error!

Part a) JOURNAL ENTRIES:

Maarten's Animal Hospital Incorporated – General Journal

	$	$

	$	$

Computation:

	$	$

	$	$

	$	$

Computation:

	$	$

	$	$

	$	$

	$	$

Computation:

	$	$

	$	$

	$	$

	$	$

Part b) POSTING TO THE LEDGER:

Maarten's Animal Hospital Incorporated – General Ledger

Part c) PREPARING THE UNADJUSTED TRIAL BALANCE:

Maarten's Animal Hospital Incorporated
Unadjusted Trial Balance

Account	Debit $	Credit $
TOTAL		

Part d) ADJUSTING and OTHER ENTRIES:

Maarten's Animal Hospital Incorporated – General Journal

	$	$

Computations:

	$	$

Computations:

	$	$

Computations:

	$	$

Computations:

	$	$

Computations:

	$	$

Computations:

	$	$

Maarten's Animal Hospital Incorporated – General Ledger (partial)

Note: Sufficient ledger space is provided for each T-account needed. Not all are adjusting entries. You will have to bring the account name and balance forward, where appropriate.

Part e) ADJUSTED TRIAL BALANCE:

Maarten's Animal Hospital Incorporated
Adjusted Trial Balance

Account	Debit $	Credit $

TOTAL		

Part f) FINANCIAL STATEMENTS:

Maarten's Animal Hospital Incorporated
Income Statement

____

Operating Expenses:		
Total Operating Expenses		
Operating Income		
Income before Income Taxes		
Income Tax Expense (30%)		
Net Income		

Part g) CLOSING ENTRIES:

Maarten's Animal Hospital Incorporated
Balance Sheet

____

ASSETS	$
TOTAL ASSETS	
LIABILITIES	
Current Liabilities	
Total Current Liabilities	
Total Liabilities	
OWNERS' EQUITY	
Total Owners' Equity	
TOTAL LIABILITIES AND OWNERS' EQUITY	

Part g) CLOSING ENTRIES:

First, the Adjusting Entry for Income Taxes:

Maarten's Animal Hospital Incorporated – General Journal

	$	$

Computation:

Next, all the Closing Entries:

Maarten's Animal Hospital Incorporated – General Journal

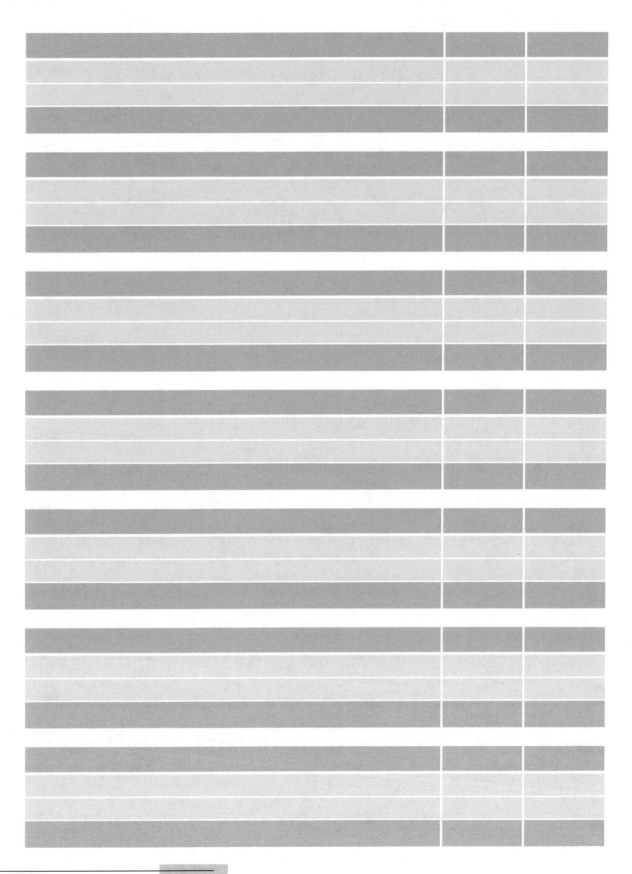

Maarten's Animal Hospital Incorporated – General Ledger

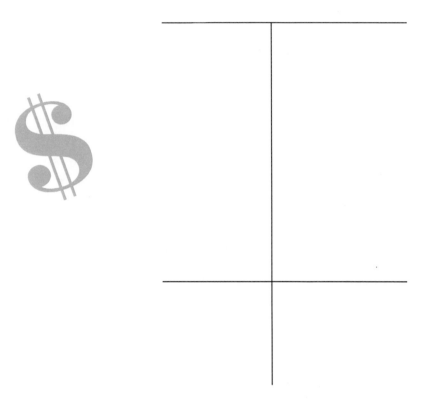

Part h) POST-CLOSING TRIAL BALANCE:

Maarten's Animal Hospital Incorporated
Post-Closing Trial Balance

Account	Debit $	Credit $
TOTAL		

Part i) Financial statement preparation question:

Evaluate the accounting methods used by Jay Byrd.

____

____

____

____

____

____

Solution to Case One

Part a) JOURNAL ENTRIES:

Maarten's Animal Hospital Incorporated – General Journal

Transaction # 1	$	$
Medical Supplies Inventory	*50,000*	
Accounts Payable		*50,000*
To record the purchase of $50,000 of medical supplies on account.		

Transaction #2	$	$
Cash	*189,000*	
Accounts Receivable	*361,000*	
Sales Revenue		*550,000*
To record the sales for the third quarter.		

Computation:
$550,000 - $361,000 = $189,000.

Transaction #3	$	$
Salaries Expense	*150,000*	
Salaries Payable		*150,000*
To record the salaries expense incurred during the third quarter.		

Transaction #3	$	$
Wages Expense	42,000	
Wages Payable		42,000
To record the wages expense incurred during the third quarter.		

Transaction #3	$	$
Wages Payable	80,000*	
Salaries Payable	240,000**	
Cash		320,000
To record the salaries and wages paid during the third quarter.		

Computation:

*The wages payable at the end of June plus the wage expense for the third quarter amount to $38,000 + $42,000 = $80,000.

**The balance is paid to salaries owing: $320,000 - $80,000 = $240,000.

Transaction #4	$	$
Cash	3,800	
Accounts Receivable		3,800
To record cash received from customers for payment on their accounts.		

Transaction #5	$	$
Accounts Payable	90,500	
Cash		90,500
To record payment on account to suppliers.		

Transaction # 6	$	$
Land	70,000	
Real Estate		70,000
To close the improper account Real Estate and open the Land account.		

Transaction # 6	$	$
Building	*420,000*	
Real Estate		*420,000*
To close the improper account Real Estate and open the Building account.		

Computation:

$490,000 - $70,000 = $420,000.

Transaction # 7	$	$
Repairs and Maintenance Expense	*5,400*	
Cash		*5,400*
To record the cash payment of repairs and maintenance.		

Transaction # 7	$	$
Building	*15,000*	
Cash		*15,000*
To record the real estate commission associated with the purchase of the building.		

Transaction # 7	$	$
Miscellaneous Expense	*6,900*	
Cash		*6,900*
To record the cash payment of miscellaneous expenses.		

Computations:

$27,300 - $5,400 - $15,000 = $6,900 in "true" miscellaneous expenses.

Transaction # 8	$	$
Cash	*260,000*	
Temporary Investments		*250,300*
Gain on Sale of Temporary Investments		*9,700*
To record the disposal and gain on the sale of temporary investments.		

Computations:

$260,000 - $250,300 = $9,700 gain.

Part b) POSTING TO THE LEDGER:

Maarten's Animal Hospital Incorporated – General Ledger

Cash

Bal. 25,500	320,000(#3)
(#2) 189,000	
(#4) 3,800	90,500 (#5)
	5,400 (#7)
	15,000 (#7)
(#8)260,000	6,900(#7)
Bal. 40,500	

Accounts Receivable

Bal. 4,800	3,800 (#4)
(#2) 361,000	
Bal. 362,000	

Temporary Investments

Bal. 250,300	250,300 (#8)
Bal. 0	

Medical Supplies Inventory

Bal. 226,000	
(#1) 50,000	
Bal. 276,000	

Prepaid Insurance

Bal. 30,000	

Equipment

Bal. 590,000	

Accumulated Depreciation (Equipment)

	162,000 Bal.

Real Estate

Bal. 490,000	70,000 (#6)
	420,000 (#6)
Bal. 0	

Building

(#6) 420,000	
(#7) 15,000	
Bal. 435,000	

Land

(#6) 70,000	

Accounts Payable

(#5) 90,500	89,200 Bal.
	50,000 (#1)
	48,700 Bal.

Salaries Payable

(#2) 240,000	150,000 Bal.
	150,000(#3)
	60,000 Bal.

Wages Payable

(#3) 80,000	38,000 Bal.
	42,000 (#3)
	Bal. 0

Income Taxes Payable

	32,500 Bal.

Note Payable (long-term)

	135,000 Bal.

Common Share Capital

	300,000 Bal.

Retained Earnings

	709,900 Bal.

Sale Revenue

	550,000 (#2)

Salaries Expense

(#3) 150,000	

Wages Expense

(#3) 42,000	

Repairs and Maintenance Expense

(#7) 5,400	

Miscellaneous Expense

(#7) 6,900	

Gain on Sale of Temporary Investments

	(#8) 9,700

Part c) PREPARING THE UNADJUSTED TRIAL BALANCE:

Maarten's Animal Hospital Incorporated
Unadjusted Trial Balance
As at September 30, 2014

Account	Debit $	Credit $
Cash	40,500	
Accounts Receivable	362,000	
Medical Supplies Inventory	276,000	
Prepaid Insurance	30,000	
Equipment	590,000	
Accumulated Depreciation (Equipment)		162,000
Building	435,000	
Land	70,000	
Accounts Payable		48,700
Salaries Payable		60,000
Income Taxes Payable		32,500
Note Payable (long-term)		135,000
Common Share Capital		300,000
Retained Earnings		709,900
Sales Revenue		550,000
Salaries Expense	150,000	
Wages Expense	42,000	
Repairs and Maintenance Expense	5,400	
Miscellaneous Expense	6,900	
Gain on Sale of Temporary Investments		9,700
TOTAL	2,007,800	2,007,800

Part d) ADJUSTING and OTHER ENTRIES:

Maarten's Animal Hospital Incorporated – General Journal

September 30, 2014 – Transaction #9	$	$
Insurance Expense	*7,500*	
Prepaid Insurance		*7,500*
To record the insurance expense for the third quarter.		

Computations:
$30,000 ÷ 4 = $7,500 per quarter or every three months.

September 30, 2014 – Transaction #10	$	$
Depreciation Expense (Equipment)	*9,000*	
Accumulated Depreciation (Equipment)		*9,000*
To record the depreciation expense for the equipment for the third quarter.		

Computations:
($590,000 - $50,000) ÷ 15 years = $36,000 per year.
$36, 000 ÷ 4 = $9,000 per quarter (or every three months).

September 30, 2014 – Transaction #11	$	$
Depreciation Expense (Building)	*5,438*	
Accumulated Depreciation (Building)		*5,438*
To record the depreciation expense for the building for the third quarter		

Computations:
($435,000) x 5% = $21,750 per year.
$21,750 ÷ 4 = $5,437.50 or $5,438 per quarter (or every three months).

September 30, 2014 – Transaction #12	$	$
Medical Supplies Expense	*209,000*	
Medical Supplies Inventory		*209,000*
To record the medical supplies used during the third quarter.		

Computations:
$276,000 - $67,000 = $209,000.

September 30 – Transaction #13	$	$
Note Payable	7,500	
Interest Expense (long-term)	2,700	
Interest Payable		2,700
Cash		7,500
To record the quarterly payment on the installment loan and the interest expense incurred, but not yet paid.		

Computations:

$30,000 ÷ 4 = $7,500 per quarter (or every three months).

*$135,000 x 8% x 1/4 = $2,700 interest expense for the third quarter.

*$15,000 had been paid for the 1st + 2nd quarter.

September 30, 2014 – Transaction #14	$	$
Common Share Capital	90,000	
Preferred Share Capital		90,000
Retained Earnings	3,000	
Preferred Dividend Payable		3,000
To remove the preferred share equity from the common share equity account and record the cumulative preferred share dividend declared but not yet paid.		

Computations:

1,000 x $90 = $90,000.

1,000 x $3.00 = $3,000.

September 30, 2014 – Transaction #15	$	$
Income Taxes Payable	30,000	
Cash		30,000
To record the payment of the quarterly installment for income taxes.		

Note: this is not an adjusting entry as the cash account was involved. The adjusting entry needed to record this quarter's income tax expense will be prepared with the closing entries.

Maarten's Animal Hospital Incorporated – General Ledger (partial)

Prepaid Insurance

Bal. 30,000	7,500 (#9)
Bal. 22,500	

Insurance Expense

(#9) 7,500	

Accumulated Depreciation (Equipment)

	162,000 Bal.
	9,000 (#10)
	171,000 Bal.

Depreciation Expense (Equipment)

(#10) 9,000	

Accumulated Depreciation (Building)

	5,438 (#11)
	5,438 Bal.

Depreciation Expense (Building)

(#11) 5,438	

Medical Supplies Inventory

Bal. 276,000	
	209,000 (#12)
Bal. 67,000	

Medical Supplies Expense

(#12) 209,000	

Note Payable (long-term)

	135,000 Bal.
(#13) 7,500	
	127,500 Bal.

Interest Expense (long-term)

(#13) 2,700	

Interest Payable

	2,700 (#13)

Cash

Bal. 40,500	7,500 (#13)
	30,000 (#15)
Bal. 3,000	

Preferred Share Capital

	90,000 (#14)

Preferred Dividend Payable

	3,000 (#14)

Income Taxes Payable

	32,500 Bal.
(#15) 30,000	
	2,500 Bal.

Common Share Capital

	300,000 Bal.
(#14) 90,000	
	210,000 Bal.

Retained Earnings

	709,900 Bal.
(#14) 3,000	
	706,900

Part e) ADJUSTED TRIAL BALANCE:

Maarten's Animal Hospital Incorporated
Adjusted Trial Balance
September 30, 2014

Account	Debit $	Credit $
Cash	3,000	
Accounts Receivable	362,000	
Medical Supplies Inventory	67,000	
Prepaid Insurance	22,500	
Equipment	590,000	
Accumulated Depreciation (Equipment)		171,000
Building	435,000	
Accumulated Depreciation (Building)		5,438
Land	70,000	
Accounts Payable		48,700
Salaries Payable		60,000
Preferred Dividend Payable		3,000
Interest Payable		2,700
Income Taxes Payable		2,500
Note Payable (long-term)		127,500
Preferred Share Capital		90,000
Common Share Capital		210,000
Retained Earnings		706,900
Sales Revenue		550,000
Medical Supplies Expense	209,000	
Salaries Expense	150,000	
Wages Expense	42,000	
Insurance Expense	7,500	
Repairs and Maintenance Expense	5,400	
Depreciation Expense (Equipment)	9,000	
Depreciation Expense (Building)	5,438	
Miscellaneous Expense	6,900	
Interest Expense (long-term)	2,700	
Gain on Sale of Temporary Investments		9,700
TOTAL	1,987,438	1,987,438

Part f) FINANCIAL STATEMENTS:

Maarten's Animal Hospital Incorporated
Income Statement
For three months ending September 30, 2014

Sales Revenue		$550,000
Operating Expenses:		
Medical Supplies Expense	$209,000	
Salaries Expense	150,000	
Wages Expense	42,000	
Insurance Expense	7,500	
Repairs and Maintenance Expense	5,400	
Depreciation Expense (Equipment)	9,000	
Depreciation Expense (Building)	5,438	
Miscellaneous Expense	6,900	
Total Operating Expenses		(435,238)
Operating Income		114,762
Gain on Sale of Temporary Investments		9,700*
Interest Expense, long-term debt		(2,700)
Income before Income Taxes		121,762
Income Tax Expense (30%)		36,529
Net Income		**$85,233**

*we will ignore the true tax treatment of this realized holding gain.

Maarten's Animal Hospital Incorporated
Balance Sheet
As at September 30, 2014

ASSETS		$
Cash		3,000
Accounts Receivable		362,000
Medical Supplies Inventory		67,000
Prepaid Insurance		22,500
Equipment	590,000	
Less: Accumulated Depreciation	(171,000)	419,000
Building	435,000	
Less: Accumulated Depreciation	(5,438)	429,562
Land		70,000
TOTAL ASSETS		1,373,062
LIABILITIES		
Current Liabilities		
Accounts Payable		48,700
Salaries Payable		60,000
Preferred Dividend Payable		3,000
Interest Payable		2,700
Income Taxes Payable*		39,029
Total Current Liabilities		**153,429**
Note Payable (5 years)		127,500
Total Liabilities		**280,929**
OWNERS' EQUITY		
Preferred Share Capital		90,000
Common Share Capital		210,000
Retained Earnings**		792,133
Total Owners' Equity		**1,092,133**
TOTAL LIABILITIES AND OWNERS' EQUITY		1,373,062

*Income Taxes Payable includes Income Tax Expense for the third quarter: $2,500 + $36,529 = $39,029 (see adjusting entry with closing entries below).
**$706,900 + $85,233 = $792,133.

NOTE: *the order of assets on the balance sheet is according to their liquidity. Also, details regarding the preferred and common shares (characteristics, number authorized and outstanding, etc.) would be presented.*

Part g) CLOSING ENTRIES:

First, the Adjusting Entry for Income Taxes:

Maarten's Animal Hospital Incorporated – General Journal

September 30, 2014- Transaction #15	*$*	*$*
Income Tax Expense	*36,529*	
Income Taxes Payable		*36,529*
To record the income tax expense for the third quarter.		

Computation: *obtained from the Income Statement.*

Next, all the Closing Entries:

September 30, 2014	*$*	*$*
Sales Revenue	*550,000*	
Income Summary		*550,000*
To close Sales Revenue to Income Summary.		

September 30, 2014	*$*	*$*
Income Summary	*209,000*	
Medical Supplies Expense		*209,000*
To close Medical Supplies Expense to Income Summary.		

September 30, 2014	*$*	*$*
Income Summary	*150,000*	
Salaries Expense		*150,000*
To close Salaries Expense to Income Summary.		

September 30, 2014	$	$
Income Summary	42,000	
Wages Expense		42,000
To close Wages Expense to Income Summary.		

September 30, 2014	$	$
Income Summary	7,500	
Insurance Expense		7,500
To close Insurance Expense to Income Summary.		

September 30, 2014	$	$
Income Summary	5,400	
Repairs and Maintenance Expense		5,400
To close Repairs and Maintenance Expense to Income Summary.		

September 30, 2014	$	$
Income Summary	9,000	
Depreciation Expense (Equipment)		9,000
To close Depreciation Expense (Equipment) to Income Summary.		

September 30, 2014	$	$
Income Summary	5,438	
Depreciation Expense (Building)		5,438
To close Depreciation Expense (Building) to Income Summary.		

September 30, 2014	$	$
Income Summary	6,900	
Miscellaneous Expense		6,900
To close Miscellaneous Expense to Income Summary.		

September 30, 2014	$	$
Income Summary	2,700	
Interest Expense (long-term)		2,700
To close Interest Expense to Income Summary.		

September 30, 2014	$	$
Gain on Sale of Temporary Investments	9,700	
Income Summary		9,700
To close Gain on Sale of Temporary Investments to Income Summary.		

September 30, 2014	$	$
Income Summary	36,529	
Income Tax Expense		36,529
To close Income Tax Expense to Income Summary.		

September 30, 2014	$	$
Income Summary	85,233	
Retained Earnings		85,233
To close Income Summary to Retained Earnings.		

Posting to the Ledger: NOTE: The first balances shown are from the Adjusted Trial Balance.

Maarten's Animal Hospital Incorporated – General Ledger

Cash	
Bal. 3,000	

Accounts Receivable	
Bal. 362,000	

Medical Supplies Inventory	
Bal. 67,000	

Prepaid Insurance	
Bal. 22,500	

Equipment	
Bal. 590,000	

Accumulated Depreciation (Equipment)	
	171,000 Bal.

Building

Bal. 435,000	

Accumulated Depreciation (Building)

	5,438 Bal.

Land

(#6) 70,000	

Accounts Payable

	48,700 Bal.

Salaries Payable

	60,000 Bal.

Preferred Dividend Payable

	3,000 Bal.

Interest Payable

	2,700 Bal.

Income Taxes Payable

	2,500 Bal.
	36,529 (adj.)
	39,029 Bal.

Note Payable (long-term)

	127,500 Bal.

Preferred Share Capital

	90,000 Bal.

Common Share Capital

	210,000 Bal.

Retained Earnings

	706,900 Bal.
85,233 (close)	
	792,133 Bal.

Sale Revenue

Close 550,000	550,000 Bal.

Medical Supplies Expense

Bal. 209,000	209,000 close

Salaries Expense

Bal. 150,000	150,000 close

Wages Expense

Bal. 42,000	42,000 close

Insurance Expense

Bal. 7,500	7,500 close

Repairs Maintenance Expense

Bal. 5,400	5,400 close

Depreciation Expense (Equipment)

Bal. 9,000	9,000 close

Depreciation Expense (Building)

Bal. 5,438	5,438 close

Miscellaneous Expense

Bal. 6,900	6,900 close

Interest Expense (long-term)

Bal. 2,700	2,700 close

Gain on Sale of Temporary Investments

close 9,700	9,700 Bal.

Income Tax Expense

36,529	36,529 close

Income Summary

		550,000	Sales
Med. Supplies	209,000		
Salaries	150,000		
Wages	42,000		
Insurance	7,500		
Repairs	5,400		
Depreciation	9,000		
Depreciation	5,438		
Miscellaneous	6,900		
Interest Expense	2,700	9,700	Realized Gain
Income Tax	36,529		
		85,233	Bal.
			Note: this is Net Income, we credit it to Retained Earnings
Close 85,233			

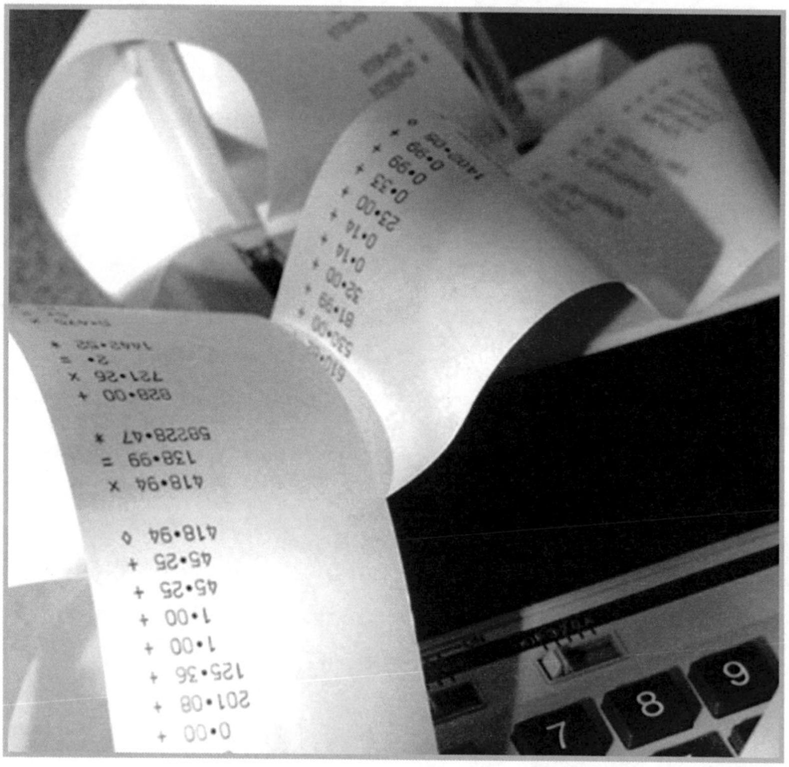

Part h) POST-CLOSING TRIAL BALANCE:

Maarten's Animal Hospital Incorporated
Post-Closing Trial Balance
As at September 30, 2014

Account	Debit $	Credit $
Cash	3,000	
Accounts Receivable	362,000	
Medical Supplies Inventory	67,000	
Prepaid Insurance	22,500	
Equipment	590,000	
Accumulated Depreciation (Equipment)		171,000
Building	435,000	
Accumulated Depreciation (Building)		5,438
Land	70,000	
Accounts Payable		48,700
Salaries Payable		60,000
Preferred Dividend Payable		3,000
Interest Payable		2,700
Income Taxes Payable		39,029
Note Payable (long-term)		127,500
Preferred Share Capital		90,000
Common Share Capital		210,000
Retained Earnings		792,133
TOTAL	1,549,500	1,549,500

Part i) Financial statement preparation question:

Evaluate the accounting methods used by Jay Byrd.

Jay Byrd broke the generally accepted accounting principles several times when preparing the financial reports for Maarten's Animal Hospital. The main criticisms are as follows:

- *The Real Estate account created did not separate land from building. This would make depreciation on the building difficult to assess. Furthermore, it appears he did not plan to depreciate the building.*
- *The Miscellaneous Expenses contained Repairs and Maintenance Expenses and Real Estate Expenses. They must be accounted for separately. Furthermore, as the Real Estate Expense was tied to the purchase of the property it should be capitalized with the Building account, not expensed to the income statement.*
- *The Note Payable was probably reported as a current liability (notice the position of the account in the post-closing trial balance prepared by Mr. Byrd as at June 30, 2014). With a maturity of five years it is clearly a long-term liability.*
- *Preferred Equity must be shown separately from Common Equity. Jay Byrd lumped them together in the Common Share Capital account.*
- *Finally, Jay Byrd did not take his professional duties seriously. He left for vacation before ensuring someone was available to close the books at the end of the quarter and prepare the financial statements.*

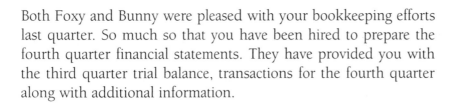

Case Two

Maarten's Animal Hospital - Fourth Quarter 2014

Foxy was less than impressed when Jay Byrd left for holidays without completing the third quarter financial reports. She was further distressed to find his accounting skills were not as topnotch as she had been led to believe. When Jay returned from holidays, Foxy informed him his services would no longer be needed.

Both Foxy and Bunny were pleased with your bookkeeping efforts last quarter. So much so that you have been hired to prepare the fourth quarter financial statements. They have provided you with the third quarter trial balance, transactions for the fourth quarter along with additional information.

Maarten's Animal Hospital Incorporated
Post-Closing Trial Balance
As at September 30, 2014

Account	Debit $	Credit $
Cash	3,000	
Accounts Receivable	362,000	
Medical Supplies Inventory	67,000	
Prepaid Insurance	22,500	
Equipment	590,000	
Accumulated Depreciation (Equipment)		171,000
Building	435,000	
Accumulated Depreciation (Building)		5,438
Land	70,000	
Accounts Payable		48,700
Salaries Payable		60,000
Preferred Dividend Payable		3,000
Interest Payable		2,700
Income Taxes Payable		39,029

Note Payable (long-term)		127,500
Preferred Share Capital		90,000
Common Share Capital		210,000
Retained Earnings		792,133
TOTAL	1,549,500	1,549,500

Transactions during the fourth quarter and additional information are as follows: (note some transactions may require more than one journal entry)

1. Purchased $150,000 worth of medical supplies during the quarter, on account. The terms of sale were 1/15 net 30. The account was paid in full during the discount period.
2. Purchased a new machine in exchange for a non-interest-bearing note at the beginning of November. The invoice price of the equipment was $87,000. The face value of the note is $93,525. Its maturity is nine months. Note: Do not capitalize the interest as part of the machine account.
3. Sales for the quarter were $565,000 of which $172,000 were on account.
4. The salaries expense is $150,000 each quarter. The wage expense for the third quarter is $45,500. Total cash paid to employees during the quarter is $150,000. Wages are always paid in full before salaries.
5. Various credit customers pay a total of $315,800 on their accounts during the quarter.
6. Maarten's Animal Hospital pays $20,300 to its suppliers for accounts payable.
7. Two- thousand no-par common shares are sold to Foxy's brother, Robin Maarten at a price of $20 each, in exchange for cash.
8. Repairs and maintenance to the equipment cost $6,000 for the quarter. Delivery and set-up charges for the new machine cost $2,350. Miscellaneous expenses amount to $7,300. All of these amounts are paid in cash.
9. If the cash account exceeds $100,000 during the quarter, the excess amount is invested in Temporary Investments.

Information relating to adjusting and other entries required at the end of the quarter is as follows:

10. The premium on a one-year insurance policy for the year July 1, 2014 to June 30, 2015 had been paid in full on June 30, 2014.

11. The new machine is expected to have a useful life of 20 years, after which time it will cost $4,500 to dispose of- a "negative" salvage. The machine was purchased on November 1, 2014.

12. The equipment, not the new machine, is expected to become obsolete earlier than originally planned. Its useful life has been shortened to 10 years starting October 1, 2014, and the estimated salvage value has been reduced to $25,000. This equipment is depreciated by using the straight-line method.

13. The building should be depreciated using the declining balance method at a 5% rate.

14. A physical count at the end of December showed there was $45,000 in medical supplies on hand.

15. On January 1, 2014 a five-year Note Payable with annual interest calculated at 8%, and principal repayment installments of $30,000 per year, was issued. Maarten's Animal Hospital makes a cash installment payment to the bank at the end of each quarter for principal repayment (equal amounts each quarter), and a cash interest payment every six months (at the end of the second and fourth quarters). Note that any interest expense incurred on the short-term note must also be reported.

16. If there was sufficient cash to purchase Temporary Investments during the quarter, then Preferred Dividends are declared and paid (together with any dividends owing from the preceding quarter).

17. On the last day of each quarter the company makes a cash income tax payment of $30,000 regardless of the actual income tax expense. Maarten's Animal Hospital is subject to an Income Tax rate of 30%.

Today is December 31, 2014. In order to close the books for the fourth quarter of 2014 you are required to do the following:

a. Prepare the journal entries to record the transactions for this quarter. The transactions have been accumulated so instead of recording the date, use the transaction number provided.

b. Set up T-accounts and enter the opening balances in the accounts from September 30, 2014. Post the entries from part a) to the T-accounts, creating new ones as needed. Use the transaction numbers as a reference.

c. Prepare an unadjusted Trial Balance as of December 31, 2014.

d. Prepare the adjusting and other entries required at the end of December. Post them to their T-accounts.

e. Prepare an adjusted Trial Balance as of December 31, 2014.

f. Prepare the financial statements for the month of December.

g. Prepare and post the Closing Entries.

h. Prepare a Post-Closing Trial Balance.

We have provided space to complete this work. Using these forms will help guide you through all the steps. If you have any space leftover then you have probably made an error!

Part a) JOURNAL ENTRIES:

Maarten's Animal Hospital Incorporated – General Journal

Transaction #	$	$

Computation:

Transaction #	$	$

Computation:

Transaction #	$	$

Computation:

Transaction #	$	$

Transaction #	$	$

Transaction #	$	$

Computation:

Transaction #	$	$

Transaction #	$	$

Transaction #	$	$

Computation:

Transaction #	$	$

Transaction #	$	$

Transaction #	$	$

Transaction #	$	$

Computations:

Part b) POSTING TO THE LEDGER:

Maarten's Animal Hospital Incorporated – General Ledger

Part c) PREPARING THE UNADJUSTED TRIAL BALANCE:

Maarten's Animal Hospital Incorporated
Unadjusted Trial Balance

____

Account	Debit $	Credit $
TOTAL		

Part d) ADJUSTING and OTHER ENTRIES:

Maarten's Animal Hospital Incorporated – General Journal

	$	$

Computations:

	$	$

Computations:

	$	$

Computations:

	$	$

Computations:

	$	$

Computations:

	$	$

Computations:

	$	$

Computations:

	$	$

Computations:

	$	$

Maarten's Animal Hospital Incorporated – General Ledger (partial)

Note: Sufficient ledger space is provided for each T-account needed. Not all are adjusting entries. You will have to bring the account name and balance forward, where appropriate.

Part e) ADJUSTED TRIAL BALANCE:

Maarten's Animal Hospital Incorporated
Adjusted Trial Balance

____

Account	Debit $	Credit $
TOTAL		

Part f) FINANCIAL STATEMENTS:

Maarten's Animal Hospital Incorporated
Income Statement

Operating Expenses:		
Total Operating Expenses		
Operating Income		
Income before Income Taxes		
Income Tax Expense (30%)		
Net Income		

Maarten's Animal Hospital Incorporated
Balance Sheet

ASSETS	$
TOTAL ASSETS	
LIABILITIES	
Current Liabilities	
Total Current Liabilities	
Total Liabilities	
OWNERS' EQUITY	
Total Owners' Equity	
TOTAL LIABILITIES AND OWNERS' EQUITY	

Part g) CLOSING ENTRIES:

First, the Adjusting Entry for Income Taxes:

Maarten's Animal Hospital Incorporated – General Journal

	$	$

Computation:

Next, all the Closing Entries:

	$	$

	$	$

	$	$

	$	$

	$	$

	$	$

	$	$

	$	$

	$	$

	$	$

	$	$

	$	$

	$	$

	$	$

Posting to the Ledger: NOTE: You should first post the balances from the Adjusted Trial Balance.

Maarten's Animal Hospital Incorporated – General Ledger

Income Summary

Part h) POST-CLOSING TRIAL BALANCE:

Maarten's Animal Hospital Incorporated
Post-Closing Trial Balance

____

Account	Debit $	Credit $
TOTAL		

Solution to Case Two

Part a) JOURNAL ENTRIES:

Maarten's Animal Hospital Incorporated – General Journal

Transaction # 1	$	$
Medical Supplies Inventory	148,500	
Cash		148,500
To record the purchase of $150,000 of medical supplies paid for in cash, with a 1% discount.		

Computation:
$150,000 x 1% = $1,500.
$150,000 - $1,500 = $148,500.

Transaction #2	$	$
Machine	87,000	
Discount on Note Payable (short-term)	6,525	
Note Payable (short-term)		93,525
To record the purchase of a machine in exchange for a noninterest-bearing note, due in nine months.		

Computation:
$93,525 - $87,000 = $6,525.

Transaction #3	$	$
Cash	393,000	
Accounts Receivable	172,000	
Sales Revenue		565,000
To record the sales revenue earned during the fourth quarter.		

Computation:
$565,000 - $172,000 = $393,000.

Transaction #4	$	$
Salaries Expense	150,000	
Salaries Payable		150,000
To record the salaries expense incurred during the fourth quarter.		

Transaction #4	$	$
Wages Expense	45,500	
Cash		45,500
To record the wages expense incurred and paid during the fourth quarter.		

Transaction #4	$	$
Salaries Payable	104,500	
Cash		104,500
To record the salaries paid during the fourth quarter.		

Computation:

After the fourth quarter wages are paid there is $104,500 available to pay salaries ($150,000 - $45,500).

Transaction #5	$	$
Cash	315,800	
Accounts Receivable		315,800
To record cash received from customers for payment on their accounts.		

Transaction #6	$	$
Accounts Payable	20,300	
Cash		20,300
To record payment on account to suppliers.		

Transaction # 7	$	$
Cash	40,000	
Common Share Capital		40,000
To record the sale of 2,000 no-par common shares to Robin Maarten at $20 each.		

Computation:

2,000 x $20 = $40,000.

Transaction # 8	$	$
Repairs and Maintenance Expense	6,000	
Cash		6,000
To record the cash payment of repairs and maintenance.		

Transaction # 8	$	$
Machine	2,350	
Cash		2,350
To record the delivery and set-up charges associated with the new machine.		

Transaction # 8	$	$
Miscellaneous Expense	7,300	
Cash		7,300
To record the cash payment of miscellaneous expenses.		

Transaction # 9	$	$
Temporary Investments	317,350	
Cash		317,350
To record the purchase of Temporary Investments with excess cash.		

Computations:

$3,000 - $148,500 + $393,000 - $45,500 - $104,500 + $315,800 - $20,300 + $40,000 - $6,000 - $2,350 - $7,300 = $417,350.

$417,350 - $100,000 = $317,350.

Part b) POSTING TO THE LEDGER:

Maarten's Animal Hospital Incorporated – General Ledger

Cash

Bal. 3,000	148,500 (#1)
(#3) 393,000	45,500 (#4)
(#5) 315,800	104,500 (#4)
	20,300 (#6)
(#7) 40,000	
	6,000 (#8)
	2,350 (#8)
	7,300 (#8)
Bal. 417,350	
	317,350 (#9)
Bal. 100,000	

Accounts Receivable

Bal. 362,000	315,800 (#5)
(#2) 172,000	
Bal. 218,200	

Temporary Investments

(#9) 317,350	

Medical Supplies Inventory

Bal. 67,000	
(#1) 148,500	
Bal. 215,500	

Prepaid Insurance

Bal. 22,500	

Equipment

Bal. 590,000	

Accumulated Depreciation (Equipment)

	171,000 Bal.

Machinery

(#2) 87,000	
(#8) 2,350	
Bal. 89,350	

Building

Bal. 435,000	

Accumulated Depreciation (Building)

	5,438 Bal.

Land

Bal. 70,000	

Accounts Payable

(#6) 20,300	48,700 Bal.
	28,400 Bal.

Salaries Payable

(#4) 104,500	60,000 Bal.
	150,000(#4)
	105,500 Bal.

Preferred Dividend Payable

	3,000 Bal.

Interest Payable

	2,700 Bal.

Income Taxes Payable

	39,029 Bal.

Note Payable (short-term)

	93,525 (#2)

Discount on Note Payable (short-term)

(#2) 6,525	

Note-Payable (long-term)

	127,500 Bal.

Preferred Share Capital

	90,000 Bal.

Common Share Capital

	210,000 Bal.
	40,000 (#7)
	250,000 Bal.

Retained Earnings

	792,133 Bal.

Sales Revenue

	565,000 (#3)

Salaries Expense

(#4) 150,000	

Wages Expense

(#4) 45,500	

Repairs Maintenance Expense

(#8) 6,000	

Miscellaneous Expense

(#8) 7,300	

Part c) PREPARING THE UNADJUSTED TRIAL BALANCE:

Maarten's Animal Hospital Incorporated
Unadjusted Trial Balance
As at December 31, 2014

Account	Debit $	Credit $
Cash	100,000	
Temporary Investments	317,350	
Accounts Receivable	218,200	
Medical Supplies Inventory	215,500	
Prepaid Insurance	22,500	
Machinery	89,350	
Equipment	590,000	
Accumulated Depreciation (Equipment)		171,000
Building	435,000	
Accumulated Depreciation (Building)		5,438
Land	70,000	
Accounts Payable		28,400
Salaries Payable		105,500
Preferred Dividend Payable		3,000
Interest Payable		2,700
Income Taxes Payable		39,029
Note Payable (short-term)		93,525
Discount on Note Payable (short-term)	6,525	
Note Payable (long-term)		127,500
Preferred Share Capital		90,000
Common Share Capital		250,000
Retained Earnings		792,133
Sales Revenue		565,000
Salaries Expense	150,000	
Wages Expense	45,500	
Repairs and Maintenance Expense	6,000	
Miscellaneous Expense	7,300	
TOTAL	**2,273,225**	**2,273,225**

Part d) ADJUSTING and OTHER ENTRIES:

Maarten's Animal Hospital Incorporated – General Journal

December 31, 2014 – Transaction #10	$	$
Insurance Expense	7,500	
Prepaid Insurance		7,500
To record the insurance expense for the fourth quarter.		

Computations:

$30,000 ÷ 4 = $7,500 per quarter, or every three months.

(Alternate calculation: $22,500 ÷ 3 quarters remaining = $7,500 per quarter.)

December 31, 2014 – Transaction #11	$	$
Depreciation Expense	782	
Accumulated Depreciation (Machinery)		782
To record the depreciation expense for the new machine for two months.		

Computations:

($89,350 + $4,500) ÷ 20 years = $4,693 per year.

$4,693 ÷ 12 = $391 per month.

$391 x 2 = $782 for November and December.

December 31, 2014 – Transaction #12	$	$
Depreciation Expense	9,850	
Accumulated Depreciation (Equipment)		9,850
To record the depreciation expense for the equipment for the fourth quarter.		

Computations:

At the beginning of the quarter there remains $419,000 ($590,000 - $171,000) to be depreciated. With the revised estimates, the depreciation expense changes to $39,400 per year, or $9,850 per quarter (see below for details).

($419,000 - $25,000) ÷ 10 years = $39,400 per year.

$39,400 ÷ 4 = $9,850 per quarter (or every three months).

December 31, 2014 – Transaction #13	$	$
Depreciation Expense	5,370	
Accumulated Depreciation (Building)		5,370
To record the depreciation expense for the building for the fourth quarter.		

Computations:

(\$435,000 - \$5,438) x 5% = \$21,478 per year.

\$21,478 ÷ 4 = \$5,370 for this quarter.

December 31, 2014 – Transaction #14	$	$
Medical Supplies Expense	170,500	
Medical Supplies Inventory		170,500
To record the medical supplies used during the fourth quarter.		

Computations:

\$215,500 - \$45,000 = \$170,500.

December 31, 2014 – Transaction #15	$	$
Note Payable (long-term)	7,500*	
Interest Expense (long-term)	2,550**	
Interest Payable	2,700	
Cash		12,750***
To record the quarterly payment on the installment loan and the interest expense incurred, and paid.		

Computations:

* \$30,000 ÷ 4 = \$7,500 per quarter (or every three months).

** \$127,500 x 8% x 1/4 = \$2,550 interest expense for the fourth quarter.

***\$7,500 + \$2,550 + \$2,700 = \$12,750.

December 31 – Transaction #15	$	$
Interest Expense (short-term)	1,450	
Discount on Note Payable (short-term)		1,450
To record the interest expense incurred on the non-interest-bearing note with a maturity of nine months.		

Computations:

\$6,525 ÷ 9 = \$725 interest per month.

\$725 x 2 months = \$1,450 for November and December.

December 31, 2014 – Transaction #16	$	$
Retained Earnings	*3,000*	
Preferred Dividend Payable	*3,000*	
Cash		*6,000*
To record payment of the preferred share dividend payable (owing from third quarter) and the dividend for this quarter.		

Computations:

$3 x 1,000 shares = $3,000 preferred dividend for the fourth quarter.

December 31, 2014 – Transaction #17	$	$
Income Taxes Payable	*$30,000*	
Cash		*30,000*
To record the quarterly installment payment for income taxes.		

Note: this is not an adjusting entry as the cash account was involved. The adjusting entry needed to record this quarter's income tax expense will be prepared with the closing entries.

Maarten's Animal Hospital Incorporated – General Ledger (partial)

Prepaid Insurance

Bal. 22,500	*7,500 (#10)*
Bal. 15,000	

Insurance Expense

(#10) 7,500	

Accumulated Depreciation (Machinery)

	0 Bal.
	782 (#11)
	782 Bal.

Depreciation Expense (Machinery)

(#11) 782	

Accumulated Depreciation (Equipment)

	171,000 Bal.
	9,850 (#12)
	180,850 Bal.

Depreciation Expense (Equipment)

(#12) 9,850	

Accumulated Depreciation (Building)

	5,438 Bal.
	5,370 (#13)
	10,808 Bal.

Depreciation Expense (Building)

(#13) 5,370	

Medical Supplies Inventory

Bal. 215,500	
	170,500 (#14)
Bal. 45,000	

Medical Supplies Expense

(#14) 170,500	

Discount on Note Payable (short-term)

Bal. 6,525	
	(#15) 1,450
Bal. 5,075	

Interest Expense (short-term)

(#15) 1,450	

Note Payable (long-term)

	127,500 Bal.
(#15) 7,500	
	120,000 Bal.

Interest Expense (long-term)

(#15) 2,550	

Interest Payable

(#15) 2,700	*2,700 Bal.*

Cash

Bal. 100,000	*12,750 (#15)*
	6,000 (#16)
	30,000 (#17)
Bal. 51,250	

Retained Earnings

	792,133 Bal.
(#16) 3,000	
	789,133 Bal.

Preferred Dividend Payable

	3,000 Bal.
(#16) 3,000	
	0 Bal.

Income Taxes Payable

	39,029 Bal.
(#17) 30,000	
	9,029 Bal.

Part e) ADJUSTED TRIAL BALANCE:

Maarten's Animal Hospital Incorporated
Adjusted Trial Balance
As at December 31, 2014

Account	Debit $	Credit $
Cash	51,250	
Temporary Investments	317,350	
Accounts Receivable	218,200	
Medical Supplies Inventory	45,000	
Prepaid Insurance	15,000	
Machinery	89,350	
Accumulated Depreciation (Machinery)		782
Equipment	590,000	
Accumulated Depreciation (Equipment)		180,850
Building	435,000	
Accumulated Depreciation (Building)		10,808
Land	70,000	
Accounts Payable		28,400
Salaries Payable		105,500
Income Taxes Payable		9,029
Note Payable (short-term)		93,525
Discount on Note Payable (short-term)	5,075	
Note Payable (long-term)		120,000
Preferred Share Capital		90,000
Common Share Capital		250,000
Retained Earnings		789,133
Sales Revenue		565,000
Medical Supplies Expense	170,500	
Salaries Expense	150,000	
Wages Expense	45,500	
Insurance Expense	7,500	
Repairs and Maintenance Expense	6,000	
Depreciation Expense (Machinery)	782	
Depreciation Expense (Equipment)	9,850	
Depreciation Expense (Building)	5,370	
Miscellaneous Expense	7,300	
Interest Expense (short-term)	1,450	
Interest Expense (long-term)	2,550	
TOTAL	2,243,027	2,243,027

Part f) FINANCIAL STATEMENTS:

Maarten's Animal Hospital Incorporated
Income Statement
For the three months ending December 31, 2014

Sales Revenue		$565,000
Operating Expenses:		
Medical Supplies Expense	$170,500	
Salaries Expense	150,000	
Wages Expense	45,500	
Insurance Expense	7,500	
Repairs and Maintenance Expense	6,000	
Depreciation Expense (Machinery)	782	
Depreciation Expense (Equipment)	9,850	
Depreciation Expense (Building)	5,370	
Miscellaneous Expense	7,300	
Total Operating Expenses		**(402,802)**
Operating Income		162,198
Interest Expense (short-term debt)		(1,450)
Interest Expense (long-term debt)		(2,550)
Income before Income Taxes		158,198
Income Tax Expense (30%)		47,459
Net Income		**$110,739**

Maarten's Animal Hospital Incorporated
Balance Sheet
As at December 31, 2014

ASSETS		$
Cash		51,250
Temporary Investments		317,350
Accounts Receivable		218,200
Medical Supplies Inventory		45,000
Prepaid Insurance		15,000
Machinery	$ 89,350	
Less: Accumulated Depreciation	(782)	88,568
Equipment	590,000	
Less: Accumulated Depreciation	(180,850)	409,150
Building	435,000	
Less: Accumulated Depreciation	(10,808)	424,192
Land		70,000
TOTAL ASSETS		**1,638,710**
LIABILITIES		
Current Liabilities		
Accounts Payable		28,400
Salaries Payable		105,500
Note Payable (9 months)	$93,525	
Less: Discount on Note Payable	(5,075)	88,450
Income Taxes Payable		56,488*
Total Current Liabilities		**278,838**
Note Payable (5 years)		120,000
Total Liabilities		**398,838**
OWNERS' EQUITY		
Preferred Share Capital		90,000
Common Share Capital		250,000
Retained Earnings**		899,872
Total Owners' Equity		**1,239,872**
TOTAL LIABILITIES AND OWNERS' EQUITY		1,638,710

**Income Taxes Payable includes Income Tax Expense for the fourth quarter: $9,029 + $47,459 = $56,488 (see adjusting entry with closing entries below).*

***$789,133 + $110,739 = $899,872.*

NOTE: *the order of assets on the balance sheet is according to their liquidity. Also, details regarding the preferred and common shares (characteristics, number authorized and outstanding, etc.) would be presented.*

Part g) CLOSING ENTRIES:

First, the Adjusting Entry for Income Taxes:

Maarten's Animal Hospital Incorporated – General Journal

December 31, 2014- Transaction #17	$	$
Income Tax Expense	47,459	
Income Taxes Payable		47,459
To record the income tax expense for the fourth quarter.		

Computation:
obtained from the Income Statement.

Next, all the Closing Entries:

December 31, 2014	$	$
Sales Revenue	565,000	
Income Summary		565,000
To close Sales Revenue to Income Summary.		

December 31, 2014	$	$
Income Summary	170,500	
Medical Supplies Expense		170,500
To close Medical Supplies Expense to Income Summary.		

December 31, 2014	$	$
Income Summary	150,000	
Salaries Expense		150,000
To close Salaries Expense to Income Summary.		

December 31, 2014	$	$
Income Summary	45,500	
Wages Expense		45,500
To close Wages Expense to Income Summary.		

December 31, 2014	$	$
Income Summary	7,500	
Insurance Expense		7,500
To close Insurance Expense to Income Summary.		

December 31, 2014	$	$
Income Summary	6,000	
Repairs and Maintenance Expense		6,000
To close Repairs and Maintenance Expense to Income Summary.		

December 31, 2014	$	$
Income Summary	782	
Depreciation Expense (Machinery)		782
To close Depreciation Expense (Machinery) to Income Summary.		

December 31, 2014	$	$
Income Summary	9,850	
Depreciation Expense (Equipment)		9,850
To close Depreciation Expense (Equipment) to Income Summary.		

December 31, 2014	$	$
Income Summary	5,370	
Depreciation Expense (Building)		5,370
To close Depreciation Expense (Building) to Income Summary.		

December 31, 2014	$	$
Income Summary	7,300	
Miscellaneous Expense		7,300
To close Miscellaneous Expense to Income Summary.		

December 31, 2014	$	$
Income Summary	1,450	
Interest Expense (short-term)		1,450
To close Interest Expense on the nine-month Note to Income Summary.		

December 31, 2014	$	$
Income Summary	2,550	
Interest Expense (long-term)		2,550
To close Interest Expense on the 5 year Note to Income Summary.		

December 31, 2014	$	$
Income Summary	47,459	
Income Tax Expense		47,459
To close Income Tax Expense to Income Summary.		

December 31, 2014	$	$
Income Summary	110,739	
Retained Earnings		110,739
To close Income Summary to Retained Earnings.		

Posting to the Ledger: NOTE: The first balances shown are from the Adjusted Trial Balance.

Maarten's Animal Hospital Incorporated – General Ledger

Cash

Bal. 51,250	

Accounts Receivable

Bal. 218,200	

Temporary Investments

Bal. 317,350	

Medical Supplies Inventory

Bal. 45,000	

Prepaid Insurance

Bal. 15,000	

Machinery

Bal. 89,350	

Accumulated Depreciation (Machinery)

	782 Bal.

Equipment

Bal. 590,000	

Accumulated Depreciation (Equipment)

	180,850 Bal.

Building

Bal. 435,000	

Accumulated Depreciation (Building)

	10,808 Bal.

Land

Bal. 70,000	

Accounts Payable

	28,400 Bal.

Salaries Payable

	105,500 Bal.

Income Taxes Payable

	9,029 Bal.
	47,459 (adj.)
	56,488 Bal.

Note Payable (short-term)

	93,525 Bal.

Discount on Note Payable (short-term)

Bal. 5,075	

Note Payable (long-term)

	120,000 Bal.

Preferred Share Capital

	90,000 Bal.

Common Share Capital

	250,000 Bal.

Retained Earnings

	789,133 Bal.
	110,739 (close)
	899,872 Bal.

Sales Revenue

close 565,000	*565,000 Bal.*

Medical Supplies Inventory

Bal. 170,500	*170,500 close*

Salaries Expense

Bal. 150,000	*150,000 close*

Wages Expense

Bal. 45,500	*45,500 close*

Insurance Expense

Bal. 7,500	*7,500 close*

Repairs Maintenance Expense

Bal. 6,000	*6,000 close*

Depreciation Expense (Machinery)

Bal. 782	*782 close*

Depreciation Expense (Equipment)

Bal. 9,850	*9,850 close*

Depreciation Expense (Building)

Bal. 5,370	*5,370 close*

Miscellaneous Expense

Bal. 7,300	*7,300 close*

Interest Expense (short-term)

Bal. 1,450	*1,450 close*

Interest Expense (long-term)

Bal. 2,550	*2,550 close*

Income Tax Expense

47,459	*47,459 close*

Income Summary

		565,000 Sales
Med. Supplies	*170,500*	
Salaries	*150,000*	
Wages	*45,500*	
Insurance	*7,500*	
Repairs	*6,000*	
Depreciation	*782*	
Depreciation	*9,850*	
Depreciation	*5,370*	
Miscellaneous	*7,300*	
Interest Expense	*1,450*	
Interest Expense	*2,550*	
Income Tax	*47,459*	
		110,739 Bal.
		Note: this is Net Income, we credit it to Retained Earnings
Close 110,739		

Part h) POST-CLOSING TRIAL BALANCE:

Maarten's Animal Hospital Incorporated
Post-Closing Trial Balance
As at December 31, 2014

Account	Debit $	Credit $
Cash	51,250	
Temporary Investments	317,350	
Accounts Receivable	218,200	
Medical Supplies Inventory	45,000	
Prepaid Insurance	15,000	
Machinery	89,350	
Accumulated Depreciation (Machinery)		782
Equipment	590,000	
Accumulated Depreciation (Equipment)		180,850
Building	435,000	
Accumulated Depreciation (Building)		10,808
Land	70,000	
Accounts Payable		28,400
Salaries Payable		105,500
Income Taxes Payable		56,488
Note Payable (short-term)		93,525
Discount on Note Payable (short-term)	5,075	
Note Payable (long-term)		120,000
Preferred Share Capital		90,000
Common Share Capital		250,000
Retained Earnings		899,872
TOTAL	1,836,225	1,836,225

Notes

Notes

Notes

Notes

Notes